THROUGH THE ARTIST'S EYES

*How Having God's Eyes Can
Set Men Free from Lust*

SCOTT J. EINIG

abbott press

Abbott Press books may be ordered through booksellers or by contacting:

Abbott Press
1663 Liberty Drive
Bloomington, IN 47403
www.abbottpress.com
Phone: 1 (866) 697-5310

ISBN: 978-1-4582-2193-3 (sc)
ISBN: 978-1-4582-2192-6 (hc)
ISBN: 978-1-4582-2191-9 (e)

Library of Congress Control Number: 2018908668

Print information available on the last page.

Abbott Press rev. date: 9/12/2018

To my parents, who always believe in me
To my brothers, who help me to be
To the artists, who helped me to see
To the Artist, who set me free

I dedicate this labor of love to thee

Contents

Acknowledgments

I'd like to thank the following people for volunteering to read my manuscript and offer feedback as this book was being written. This book would not be what it is without your honesty and generosity: Keely Mix, Steve Johnson, Jamie Adams, Blayne Greiner, Andrew Ferguson, Nahshon Graumann, and Peter Volkersz.

Thank you to all the people at Abbott Press for your support and diligence in helping me realize my vision.

I'd also like to thank my editor, Sam Severn. Your contributions helped make this book something I will always be truly proud of. I want to extend a special thanks to Sam Jolman, for granting permission to quote your wonderful article. And I want to thank Mom and Dad, for making this book happen.

Who This Book Is For

The real voyage of discovery consists not in seeking new lands, but in having new eyes.

— Marcel Proust

— I can't go back, can I?
— No. But if you could, would you really want to?

— *The Matrix*

Here a great number of disabled people used to lie—the blind, the lame, the paralyzed. One who was there had been an invalid for thirty-eight years. When Jesus saw him lying there and learned that he had been in this condition for a long time, he asked him, "Do you want to get well?"

— John 5:3-6

At the time of this writing I am 25 years old, soon to be 26. I currently live in the Pacific Northwest and have lived there my whole life. I am currently single, and have been for 25 years, soon to be 26. I have had – and still have – a lot of great and wonderful people in my life who continue to teach me indispensable lessons about the nature of living life. I don't have much, but what I do have has greater value than the contents of a bank account or the square feet of a home. I have a testimony.

My journey with Christ began at a very young age. I had the great blessing of growing up in a strong Christian home and being constantly surrounded by godly influences, friends and family alike. These served as the building blocks of my foundation of faith. From sixth grade to graduation I attended a private Christian school, and I can say in all honesty that my time there was the beginning of where I stand today as a man of God. After high school Christianity became *my* faith as opposed to the faith my friends and family practiced. At the moment my line of work is retail. The car I own is ten years old, has a good-size dent in the bumper, and has its share of tics and annoyances. I recently paid a credit card bill. I take out the trash. I get the mail. I have financial woes from time to time. I tell you all of this because I want you to see that I am your neighbor. We may have walked past one another or sat at opposite ends of a restaurant without knowing it. I don't know you, but nonetheless, I want to establish a mutual understanding: We are not so different, you and I. We have things in common. We're sinners. We're brothers.

To be honest, I think we tend to place writers of Christian living books on untrue pedestals. "This guy wrote a book about overcoming lust, so I guess he never stumbles." I want to destroy that myth before we go any farther. When I use the term "lust" in these pages, I am referring to when a man lusts after a woman. I have yet to meet a man who has never found himself in this place at certain times in his life. Though I've written a book about the tools that can help us conquer this sin, this does not mean for a minute that I wake up every day completely immune to its daily temptations. It does not mean that I have mastered for myself the principles we will be discussing. Staying pure can be very hard, my brothers. I struggle, just as you struggle. I am a fellow sinner saved by grace and trying to lead a more sinless, selfless, fearless, faith-filled life. Now that we know each other a little better, I want to let you know what to expect in the pages to come.

What many of you may be wondering is why another writer would bother writing about such subjects as sex, lust and the female body. Haven't hundreds of other writers done this already? Yes, they have. But those other writers are different from me in almost every way. They are professional psychologists/counselors with decades of experience in their fields. Others have been in ministry for just as long. Some are pastors with encyclopedic knowledge of Scripture. Many have one or multiple degrees. Almost all of them are married. The perspectives in this book about these thoroughly documented subjects are unique because none of these credentials apply to its author. I don't have as many years of life or professional experience as other writers out there.

So why should you read what I have to say? Because I have something more powerful than surveys, polls, PhDs, historical knowledge and theology, something mankind cannot and never will be able to refute. What I have is a testimony. My testimony is where this book came from. It is the product of a life already lived and a life still being lived right now. A person's testimony is not bound to logic or life experience or extensive expertise in a field of study because the One behind said testimony is not bound by such things. What God did in my past has forever shaped my future in regards to the topics of this story: my relationship with, feelings about, and attitudes towards women, women's bodies, sex, marriage, and above all, my Savior. You will see where I was led astray. You will also see how I was redeemed.

It was the *way* I was redeemed that filled me with an insatiable desire to write to my fellow brothers who continue to struggle with lust. Though God works differently with all of us and we all receive healing differently, I know God can achieve in you what he did in me: freedom. I believe what God revealed to me can lead you all to Christ in a way so vast and so deep that your lives will change forever. I believe what God did in my life can save marriages. I believe the work he did in me can serve as a guide to lasting fulfillment for all who desire it. I hope that what God did for me can open up pathways to freedom from lust in your own life.

I have written this message for men, but I believe women can glean much insight from my story, and maybe receive healing themselves. I believe we have reached a point where women have a deeper desire to know about what goes on inside the hearts and souls of men, and I think these pages will offer women some valuable insight. Our society is pure chaos when it comes to relations between the sexes. To be honest, I try hard not to think about it because it bothers me so much. Though men and women seem to be trusting one another less and less these days, it does not have to be this way. Men and women would do well to learn about each other's inner struggles instead of blindly following the naive voices of our culture that say we cannot understand each other – or that we are identical. An openness to understand what these struggles are really like can lead to what men and women need to practice towards one another every day: grace, compassion, and understanding.

My history with lust was not a struggle. That is too weak a word. It was a war. There were too many times to count when I just threw up my hands and said, "I will have to accept that this sin will be in my life forever." No doubt many of you feel the same. But one of the core reasons I've written this book is to tell you that such a belief is a lie from the pit of hell. No matter what you think or believe right now, I bring you a message of hope: you *can* live a life with not even a hint of sexual immorality. It is possible. The second part of this book explains what I learned about how to achieve such a life. Though it is far from easy, it is a life worth seeking, no matter the cost. As of now, the world – and sometimes the church – accepts a standard of mediocrity as the rule instead of the exception. A lack of accountability is everywhere. A lack of brotherhood is everywhere. Men who settle for second-best in all areas of life are far too common. We know what it feels like to settle. We know how often we want to live a life of least resistance.

But this is not who our God created us to be. You and I were not created to be mediocre, nor were we created to aspire to mediocrity. We can be more than that. We *are* more than that. I know it, and you know it, too. As men, we were created not just to aspire to greatness, but to *be* great. We can be noble. We can be honorable. We can be pure in heart, mind, body and spirit. We can be the kind of men that future men will read about years after we've passed on and say, "That's the life I want." This is who we truly are, brothers. This is you. This is me. This is how God designed us. And it's time to reclaim his design before it's too late.

So we begin.

I was young. I was fascinated. I was wounded. I was dishonorable. I was a prisoner.

And I was set free.

– February 2015

xiii

PART I: My Story

1

It all began in a doctor's lobby.

Maybe it was a doctor's office. Might have been a chiropractor (it's now a dentist office). I was twelve years old, and I was waiting in the lobby for my mom's appointment to be done. For the most part, I have never considered myself a person who gets bored easily. I can be patient when I need to be. But young boys aren't renowned for their ability to be patient, and I was no exception. To put it bluntly, I was excruciatingly bored while I sat there waiting, and I did what any person of any age does in such a situation: I looked around the room for anything to entertain me.

I got up and wandered around the lobby in search of a magazine or book of any kind. It didn't matter what it was, just something – anything – to look at. I dug around the magazine rack. Nothing. I took a peak under one of the desks by the chairs, and I found a health book resting behind some random magazines. It was fairly large in size and weight. It had plenty of pictures. Perfect. Unbeknownst to me, it was a book about women's health. Not typical reading material for a boy of twelve, but desperate times call for desperate measures. I sat down by the front door and began flipping through the pages. I can't imagine what other people in the lobby thought when they saw this little boy reading a book on women's health. I got to the halfway mark when I entered the section that talked about sex.

My eyes widened. There were pictures of male and female models posing in sex positions of various kinds, along with various pieces of information regarding sexual health. One of the images showed a male model performing cunnilingus. Being a health book, none of the images were intended to be pornographic. But that was beside the point. They were images of real women in real poses who were really naked. I had never seen a naked woman before that day. I had never seen anything related to sex before that moment in the lobby. Sex was something completely foreign to me. Seeing those images was like a lightning strike from an unknown place into my young and innocent world. My eyes must have remained quite wide as I gazed. The rest of the book's contents did not exist at that point. All I could do was look at these unclothed women. I looked for maybe half an hour before I put the book away.

For the rest of the day, my thoughts could not dwell on anything other than what I saw in that book. What I saw would not leave me for years. And it was only the beginning.

Storytellers call an episode like this a sexual awakening. Though it was, I would never refer to this incident that way. For me, it was less of a sexual awakening and more of a long fall from innocence. But that's not how I saw it back then. To my preteen mind, it was a door into a previously unknown world that had not been opened gently, but completely kicked down off its hinges. What I didn't discover until a few years later was that I never should have walked through that doorway. If I knew what had been set in motion that day – what was to come as a result – I would have run away like Joseph. Had the war never begun in the first place, I'm left with a few questions: How would my story be different? How else would I have first seen the naked female body? In art? In real life? What would have happened if I had never opened that book? What would my story be like had I been raised from boyhood in the knowledge that I now have written on my heart as a young man?

2

You can probably predict some of where this portion of my story continues.

Though the war for my soul did not officially start until age thirteen, after that day in the lobby I was overwhelmed with a kind of unquenchable curiosity. I had been exposed to the female form in a way that I had never given thought to before that day. Most boys learn about women and sex from other clueless friends or other negative, ungodly influences. I didn't have friends that spoke about these things to me. I learned about it by accident. But man, was I glad that I did. That's the best way I remember it. I was glad. I was glad that I had seen women without clothing. Their bodies were so interesting to look at, and I was more than happy to spend endless minutes doing just that. The best part was that all that good-looking female flesh was so *available*. It was easy to seek and even easier to find. It didn't matter whether the women were posing for art or for men's arousal. I just wanted to see as many naked women as I possibly could.

From time immemorial, I have always been a reader and a writer. I read a lot when I was young, and I read even more as an adult. I wrote some short stories as a kid. Before high school I even penned an 80-page tome about some time travelers who end up in the Mesozoic Era and have to fight dinosaurs. It was essentially *Jurassic Park* with the action scenes of *Mad Max: Fury Road* with the physical logistics of a Bob Clampett cartoon (what I wouldn't give to find a copy of it). Being the reader I was, I could be found haunting the libraries of Snohomish County from time to time. I spent even more time there when I began going to grade school and had all that wonderful homework to do. The library had been a part of my life since birth, but when I was entering my teenage years I discovered Barnes & Noble. At that time it was the biggest place I'd ever been to that was solely dedicated to books. It was bigger than any used bookstore or library I had ever been to, and it was pure bliss. But Barnes & Noble had something the library didn't have that made it better by far.

Every time I got the chance to go, there were two sections I would always try to seek out like a wolf circling a sheep pen: Art Technique and Love and Sex. The art books were much more accessible because I could stand there and it would look like I was looking at art to other customers around me. I saw plenty of glorious nudity at that section and I loved every glorious image. The way the models posed and stood astonished me, because I was looking at women who were willing to show every inch of themselves. I never knew women did things like that. To borrow from *Aladdin*, this was a whole new world. When I had my fill of the art books, I'd try to peruse the Love and Sex aisle. That section was much more difficult to wander through because I was way more conscientious of other people looking at me (you can't exactly mistake the *Kama Sutra* for *Treasury of the Vatican Frescoes*). I was worried they'd see what I was looking at and tell me to scram or get lost. I was much more frightened of other people at that age, and I hated getting in trouble. But I was too young to realize that I should have been far more concerned about my heart and soul being in trouble. Even if someone had told me about the internal consequences I would suffer because of what I was doing, I would not have cared. All I wanted was those pictures.

Overtime, I figured out how to look at the sex books without getting caught. The Love & Sex aisle contained a lot of books that were all photos. Such books were all about the physical pleasure of sex. Nothing health-related. All pleasure. Those were the books I sought. When I saw one I wanted, I waited till no one was down the Love & Sex aisle, then I raced over, grabbed it, and bolted over to the U.S. Military History aisle (a.k.a. an aisle not devoted to sex and therefore not suspicious). To my surprise, this routine worked quite well. Without anyone else noticing what I was up to, I feasted my eyes on a full-course buffet of full-frontal nudity and sex positions performed by real people. This was even better than the art books. I don't know how it was possible, but in that time I never saw any images of penetration. Both the men and women had their genitalia cleverly hidden by whatever poses they were performing. I was too naive to notice. All I knew was that these models were granting me a physical simulation of sex, and that they were doing it without clothes. I was intoxicated.

This cycle repeated from age thirteen to fifteen. I would do my best to find any book that showed a naked woman at the library. I would do my sneaking-a-hand-in-the-cookie-jar routine at Barnes & Noble whenever my mom dropped me off. I would also watch movies. Mercifully, my parents were ones that actually cared about what I watched. They wouldn't allow me to watch R-rated movies until I was fourteen, and only then with extreme caution and tact. Back then, seeing a movie that was rated R was a rite of passage that had an almost holy significance. To me, people who had seen one were like members of some exclusive club, a club that I was gained limited access to until I turned eighteen. Most of what I saw was PG-13. No sex scenes. But some of the movies I did see still contained scantily-clad women. Bikinis and jogging outfits and lingerie, that sort of thing. I was just as hooked on those as I was on the images in the books. They weren't naked, but at least they moved. Some of these women were far away in the various shots, so I would take my Xbox remote, press PAUSE and zoom in on the women from afar to get a better look.

This is the level I had sunk to. I wanted to see as many women in as little dress as I could without getting caught by anyone. I can only recall one time in which I was caught, and of all the people to catch me it had to be my mom. I was at Barnes & Noble, fully engaging in my routine with the sex books when Mom found me. I hid the book as if my life depended on it. I scrambled around, did a little nervous pacing, verbally trying to tell her about all the cool books I had found. I can still remember what she asked me next: "Were you looking at something you shouldn't have been looking at?" My eyes and head fell to the floor. I had no words. I was caught, and there was no way I could cover it up. Mom didn't scold me, yell at me or tell me what a terrible thing I had done. She was perfectly calm and perfectly understanding. Yet I can't remember feeling such tangible shame in all my life.

After that day, my trips to Barnes & Noble ended for some time. It was then that I, my dad and my best friend Peter read a book together called *Every Young Man's Battle*.

3

Much to my surprise, Peter was struggling with much of what I was going through myself. To me, he was always someone who seemed immune to lust and impurity. Unlike most men, lust did not appear to be an issue in his life. I was wrong. He was not at the level I had stooped to, but he still had sexual feelings that manifested into lust overtime. He had much more honor than I did, but the impure desires remained. When Dad found out about our shared struggle, the timing was just right. Dad had known about *Every Young Man's Battle* from some others in our church who had recommended it. Peter and I went to the same school and thus had the same amount of free time. So once a week, we three fellow sinners trying to walk the path of purity and righteousness went through the book.

Needless to say, it was an eye-opener. It was filled with lots of great information, but there were some stand-out words of wisdom that really resonated with me. One of the biggest was the concept of bouncing the eyes. The very minute my eyes fell across a beautiful woman – either in person or on the latest cover of *Maxim* – I had to train myself to turn away and get out of there. It was good advice for someone in my position. The other piece of wisdom that I needed to hear was practicing the act of doing whatever was necessary to beat my sex drive before it beat me. All it takes is a look, then you linger with your eyes, then the impure thoughts start to come, and eventually it affects your biological sex drive, bringing with it all those sexual urges that become increasingly difficult to ignore. It was vital for my mind to be pure, and the way to do that was to not allow anything inside that would cause that evil to re-emerge and turn into something worse. Given where I was in this season of my life, this was exactly what needed to happen within me.

After finishing the book I began to put this wisdom to the test, and I slowly began to see results. I started to have victory. I could go to Barnes & Noble and not be so easily tempted. The library didn't appeal to me anymore. I still thought about the women I had seen thus far, but I thought of them as actual people and not as mere objects that existed solely for my viewing pleasure. Peter experienced victory, too. I still recall sharing our victories with one another and the sense of righteousness that built up within us during those talks. Peter had an entire year-and-a-half in which lust was completely absent his life. Things were good.

Though I was struggling with lust, I never crossed boundaries with the various girls I knew in school. Most people in grade school acquire boyfriends or girlfriends at some point, but that was not the case with me. I had crushes here and there, but never anything more (my first actual crush was in the sixth grade. Mom recalls how I would tell her about this girl by using the words every boy says when he first experiences a longing for a woman: "I can't stop thinking about her!"). But I never experienced anything further than this.

Though I was not old enough to date when the purity movement swept the church, the effects were still prominent by the time I was old enough to date. The influential book *I Kissed Dating Goodbye* was still popular, and I was encouraged by my folks to forego dating. All of these things had an effect on my views of dating during this period. I came to believe dating was, for the most part, not a good thing. But the real reason I never dated was because of my own insecurity. I was far too unsure of and uncomfortable with myself to begin a relationship with a girl. I did everything I could to cover up the fact that I liked a girl when my friends asked me. I didn't want to be made fun of, and I didn't want drama, so I would make dumb excuses for not dating. Admitting I liked a girl to her face was equally beyond me. I never kissed. I rarely hugged. I had a lot of friends in high school who were girls, all of whom I deeply cared about and loved, and I was perfectly content with being friends.

And so nothing developed between me and any girl throughout that period.

It was a fact I didn't dwell on too much until after I fell in love with God.

4

It was the summer of 2007. I was eighteen, and I had become a high school graduate. It was just me and one of my other best friends who graduated that year. A class of two. Small school.

I was very sorry to leave that place, considering all they had given back to me and instilled in me. I can remember telling my favorite teacher how much I didn't want to leave, how much I wanted my time there to continue. She told me with a smile in her forward yet equally loving way, "It's time for you to move on." In spite of my fear of going out in the wide world, I knew she was right. I walked the aisle. I gave my speech. I did all the things high school grads do, and life was now open before me. The world of job hunting lay at my feet.

Much to my chagrin, I don't remember exactly what caused it. Maybe it was the fear of looking for work. Maybe it was knowing my time at Peaceful Glen Christian School – my safe haven – was over for good. Either way, around August of that year, I was not in a good place. To put it plainly, I was in a place mentally, emotionally and spiritually, in which I felt nothing. It was ugly. I had never *not* felt something. I was a walking void for a good portion of that month. I felt broken, like a piece of myself that I could not identify was missing. It was then that I decided to read *The Sacred Romance* by John Eldredge. Dad and I had previously read *Wild At Heart* together as a sort of man-to-man activity, and I greatly enjoyed it. I wanted to read more of his work, and that was the book I chose. Little did I know that God would use it to help usher me into the most pivotal spiritual revival of my life.

I learned about beauty and what God uses it for in our lives. I learned that God speaks to us through things like music and nature and art, that the Lord had been wooing me with beauty since the day I was born. It struck so many chords within me that at times it was overwhelming. I knew that this was what I was missing, what I was longing for. As I read on, God spoke. One day I felt him summoning me to Wallace Falls, one of the hiking trails right outside of Stevens Pass, Washington. It's a two-mile hike that has spectacular views and two amazing waterfalls up in the mountains of the Pacific Northwest.

As I hiked, my eyes were opened. Not my physical eyes, but the eyes of my heart. I was seeing and experiencing the beauty of everything around me for the first time. I walked the trail and felt the trees with my hands, feeling the moss between my fingers. I stood by the river and I actually listened to the sound of the running water, as if I had never heard a river in my life. I inhaled slowly and deeply through the nostrils with my eyes closed, taking in the mountain air like it was the very life I had been missing since the day of my birth. It was as if I had never seen these things before. Everything around me felt utterly *new*. In the mountains of the Pacific Northwest, God met me. He wooed me. And I came alive.

My Christianity was no longer a belief system I practiced when I needed to.

I now had a true relationship with God. And it was a romantic one.

5

I got a job at a large retailer in October of that year. I remember Dad telling me how proud he was that I had found a job on my own. Knowing the kind of person I am, I'm amazed that I even had the courage to go looking. Either way, I was now officially a full-time working man. Something else had changed in my life, too. Not only was I developing a work ethic and learning how the workplace feels after being in school, but I was no longer lusting after women. I had begun praying – sometimes daily – for my future wife (I had started doing this when I was 16, but I was far more intentional and serious about it when I began full-time work). I would write things I wanted to give my future spouse someday. In a short time I had become what I call a "hopeful romantic." I had hope. I've noticed that romance does that. It gives hope. I always hated the term "hopeless romantic," because true romance is anything but hopeless. That time was rich with God's love, life and blessing. And it was also during this time that the cycle began.

In my entire track record with lust up to that point, I had never struggled with masturbation. When I looked at the photos at the library and bookstore, I experienced erections and deep sexual arousal, but at the time that was enough to leave me satisfied. By this time I had also begun to have nocturnal emissions (infrequently, but they had begun nonetheless). Beyond all this, however, I could look at images and not have the urge to do anything more. Masturbation was one of those sexual boundaries that I never intended to cross. Not only did I view it as a sin, but there was something about it that made me queasy. Because of my strong commitment to these beliefs, I felt I would be immune to it. Pride took hold when I felt so good about myself for not struggling with something so prevalent among other men. Then I actually tried it. It turned out to be pretty easy. All I had to do was use memories of women I had seen that were perfectly clear in my mind. From that point, the half-dream state of nocturnal emissions ceased to be my only means of sexual release.

Through masturbation I had found a way to feel every sensation for which orgasm is legendary. And I loved it. Suddenly I was that kid from four years ago, seeking out the unclothed object of desire called *woman* and telling myself I was "just being curious." I told myself – *promised* myself – I would never masturbate again. It happened not long after. I repented with a new hope of never going back. But I went back. Soon I was going back once a week. Then it was every other day. It was so wonderful to feel the greatest physical pleasure on Earth so frequently. What was horrible was the guilt, the shame, the knowledge that what I was doing was a perversion of the very thing that God had made so beautiful in the Garden of Eden. In less than six months I had gone from being swept up in God's Romance, from knowing what it was like to experience true relationship with Christ, to wallowing in the spiritual, physical and moral decay of lust all over again. *Less than six months.*

One of the reasons men masturbate is not just to feel good physically, but to feel like men. They consume a woman's body through the eyes and act on the arousal of the imagery with masturbation, not just for the sexual high, but for the emotional high. They feel validated. That was never the case with me, at least not directly. I did it because of the sensation. There is nothing more physically pleasurable than an orgasm, and I wanted as many as possible. Up until then I just wanted to view pictures of naked women. Now I wanted sex. Masturbating was the closest I would get to physical sex with a woman. I would never go "all the way," so I masturbated instead. In late 2008 the cycle had returned. My lust would flare up every couple of days and I did next to nothing to

15

prevent it. I was legitimately sorry, I will never doubt that. I repented and sometimes I actually felt forgiven. But then another temptation would arise, and I would give into it. It was not a lasting repentance.

I never expected to look back on my Barnes & Noble escapades and wonder how it could have gotten worse than that.

But God was with me. That's what happens when you're in a romance with God. He is not one to give up on it.

I can't remember where I found it. Probably a search on Amazon. A book had come into my line of sight called *Sacred Sex* by Tim Alan Gardner. As I read about the book's content, I began to feel a holy prompting, the pull of God on my heart. I also heard some other thoughts as well, thoughts that went like this: *Scott, you're still single. Sex is intended for marriage. This book clearly won't do you any good right now. This book is not meant for you.* I ignored every voice that tried to convince me that reading this book about sex was not a good idea. I bought it. I read it. My life changed.

6

Through this new book I was reading, God took me to the act of sex itself. What I learned forever altered my view of sexual intimacy. It was no longer just this awesome thing husbands and wives did with one another. It was a holy act. It was something God created and set apart for the covenant of marriage for the purpose of bringing him glory and honor. Sex had a purpose far greater than pleasure. It was a sacrament. This was all completely foreign to me. What I was learning was transforming my very mindset and outlook on this mysterious facet of human existence called sex.

As I took in what I was reading, I noticed something odd happening in me. My desire to lust was going away. Shortly after completing the book, I experienced an unprecedented month of complete freedom. When I saw an attractive woman, my mind did not immediately turn towards the sexual as if running on assembly line mechanics. When a sex scene turned up in a movie, I looked away or left the room. I was in a state of near-constant worship. I thanked God for sex, something I had never done before. My role in honoring sex as a man was now clearly defined. I walked in the hope that sex was going to be a gift I could experience with my spouse one day. Everything that was true was my daily reality. Needless to say, it was one glorious month.

But soon after, the defining lie of the years to come found its way into my life. I did the most dangerous thing I could have done. I listened to it.

At the end of that month I began to feel the urge to lust again. The cycle was slowly returning from its dungeon, and it was about to grow even more vicious. One morning I was lying in bed and I began to think about how great it would be to wake up and see my wife next to me one day. A perfectly innocent desire. Then I began to think about how great it would be to have sex and honor God through the act and make him smile on our joy. Another pure, God-given desire. Then the memories of all the images I had allowed into my mind began to surface. I began to recall the sex scenes, and I told myself that would be me and my wife one day. Then I stopped bringing my future wife into these thoughts and just lingered over the sex scenes in my mind, remembering the sounds, the movements, the exposed naked bodies. I masturbated that morning. The cycle had come back, and it would stay there for another two years.

Even after all I had learned about sex – how beautiful and holy it is when it is practiced and enjoyed within God's sacred boundaries – I was back to doing what I had tried to avoid all over again. At this point in my sin the Internet was a prominent part of my life, and I would use it to watch sex scenes from movies or TV shows. I'd take it all in and pleasure myself. One time I did this four times in a single day. Sometimes I was scared that my lust had become an addiction. I had days of freedom, sure. But mostly the cycle had become an every-other-day event.

I didn't know true freedom again until I, Peter, and my other good friend Chris took a road trip in the summer of 2010.

7

We had mapped out a trip that would take us across the continental US all the way from Seattle, Washington to Indianapolis, Indiana. A friend of Peter's that all three of us had known in our Peaceful Glen days was getting married in Indianapolis three weeks away from our start date, and we planned to get there a few days before the wedding. I can still recall the level of excitement shared between us when we sat down and planned the trip. There was no one telling us where to go or how to travel. We weren't bound to anything other than what we wanted to do. It was *our* shared experience. Most men at that age crave a journey like that, and we had it before us.

There is a reason the symbol of the open road has achieved mythic status in American history. Few things speak of freedom so clearly. You have the whole expanse of the land before you with a path running through it, and there you are in the middle with nothing but the choice of setting out to see what the land holds in store. We set out with our supplies, our Starbucks, our cameras and our music. At last, we were free men. I realized early on that I had made my chronic traveling mistake of packing way too much. But there was one thing I did not take with me on the journey. It was the most unwanted companion in my life, and its name was Lust. I had expected Lust would take itself with me, despite the fact that I desperately wanted it gone. God had other ideas.

We had our share of hard times on the journey. I recall the time when Chris thought it would be smart to drive over sand that "looked firmer" for the car and thereby getting stuck. We got rained out of our tent – twice. We all spent much more money than we originally intended. We had to replace all four tires of Chris's car when we realized none of them contained an ounce of traction. I,

19

always the most romantic of the three of us, didn't want to go to the wedding and felt forced into it. We got on each other's nerves. We argued. Avoiding lust is fairly simple when you're in a car with two other hygiene-deprived guys with whom you're on the road for ten hours a day. But the mind is a powerful temptress.

Even amid all the driving and various traveling difficulties, I was still facing temptation. I could recall with near-flawless clarity all those alluring sex scenes with all those sounds and bodies. One time this particular sex scene I had seen would simply not leave me alone while I sat in the backseat. Though I didn't really have any opportunities to masturbate, since all three of us were rarely alone during the whole trip, I could still let those images fester in my mind. I had all the time in the world for that. But I wouldn't have it. By God's grace I was able to mentally, physically and spiritually resist lust for the entire trip. And I think I was able to do this because of what God was taking me back to.

Here I was, a young Christian man, out on the road, rarely encountering women face-to-face, removed from the distractions and routines of ordinary life. It was just me, my friends who I view as brothers, and the stunning natural creation of the Artist all around us. My physical eyes were doing only a small portion of the sightseeing. It was the eyes of my heart that were doing the real looking. Gazing out over Yosemite, standing inside the swallow-dwelling chambers of Carlsbad Caverns, driving through the barren landscapes of Death Valley – God was giving me glimpses of himself everywhere. The Romancer was calling to me, and I had no choice but to answer. At one point I found myself seated at the edge of the Grand Canyon at sunset, looking at the vastness of the land in the red and golden light, and for one of only a handful of precious moments, I wanted nothing out of life other than God himself. When a man is in that state of oneness with his God, lust is not an option. It was not an option because it did not exist.

God gave to me what I so desperately needed and still need to this day. He gave me himself. Even with the hardships thrown in, that trip was a time I would not trade for anything. It tested me, and above all, it made me feel like a man, out there in the wild and finding the God of my heart around every bend of the road.

8

When we got back, the first thing I did was go to my favorite Mexican restaurant. Mexican food is my all-time favorite cuisine, and I had missed it for almost a month. Peter and Chris and I didn't contact one another for over a month-and-a-half. We needed our space more than we needed air to breathe. And when I returned, there was something else waiting for me that I hoped would be gone.

After our journey, it was back to work, back to routines, back to the life I left behind, and back to lust. I had allowed that accursed cycle to simply step right back into my life and take up its vacant seat. It proceeded on for the rest of the year until two major life experiences came my way. First, I moved in with my grandmother. It was the first time in years that I was out of Mom and Dad's place and somewhat on my own. My grandma and I were ideal roommates. We both like our solitude, reading books, watching movies, and going out to eat when we don't feel like cooking. It was a grand living situation. The second major life change was an entire year of furthering my education. Considering the branch of education I would soon be immersed in, this was very exciting. With the guidance of my parents and some well-written letters of recommendation, I was headed for the Seattle Film Institute.

I attended film school for the entire year of 2011. The year went quick. That's what really stands out. It went *fast*. At the beginning of every school year, everyone is still their own person, still not quite sure who's going to be friends with who, still sizing one another up in a way. Starting any kind of schooling is always like that, I've noticed. But that only lasted for a short time. Soon we were all pals and fellow collaborators. All of my professors were great. I worked on projects, made friends, watched films from every decade and country. That was the year I learned how to truly *watch* a movie and pay attention to detail, to study the art of cinema at a microscopic level. It was liberating to go to a place five days a week in which everyone who went there loved cinema as deeply as I did. Graduation happened in December (in a movie theater, no less). I left with a body of work, a certificate of completion, and a great group of people I called friends. I was confident that my career as a filmmaker would be off to a solid start.

I had always assumed that after film school I would still remain close with those friends and that the collaborations would continue. A lot of the great filmmakers had similar partnerships when they got their start, and I thought I'd be no exception. For most of 2012, I worked hard to maintain those relationships, and to my shock, I was never reached out to in return. I assisted on one friend's project that year, and that was it. I tried three times to begin an internship with various production studios. None of them came to fruition. By the year's end I was no longer in contact with any of my fellow students or professors. To make things worse, I was haunted mercilessly by memories of the one truly bad experience in my year at film school. My partner on that project turned out to be one of the worst people I have ever worked with, and I carried memories of the things that were said between us like a two-ton weight. It's truly amazing how one set of bad memories can overshadow a full year of good ones (it would take three years of suffering those memories daily before I was set free by the hand of God). In all this time, my savings account dwindled from a pretty good number to hardly anything, mainly due to some poor financial decisions and lack of employment.

Things like this have the power to make or break a man, and for the most part they broke me. I lived in resignation, ignoring the fact that I was deeply hurt by these feelings of abandonment and failure. I still had a very strong relationship with Christ that had been growing stronger every year since my Great Awakening. 2012 was filled with moments that could have only been crafted by his hand. I still found beauty and romance in the things I love. I still had great people in my life. But I won't pretend that I was not profoundly disappointed and flat-out wounded by what had occurred. I felt abandoned. I felt very much alone, adrift in an ocean filled with sharks. Because of all this I allowed fear to take me. As much as I desired it, I reasoned that if I didn't pursue this film career I wouldn't be hurt. Instead of trusting the Lord to guide me into the career path I honestly wanted, I decided to use a false antidote for my pain and fear. I decided to find comfort in lust. I decided to allow the cycle to comfort me. It still lived. It lived because I allowed it to live.

9

I resumed working at the same retailer around October of 2012. Up until then I had worked in Dad's tree farm and did various jobs for my grandma to make money. Grandma wages are famously generous. But when I resumed work at the old store, saw the old faces and began making new friends, I started noticing a shift in my life.

My spiritual life in the workplace up until then had usually been fairly God-centered. I had tried to bring God to work by praying in the spirit and sometimes quietly out loud during my shift. But I now had a *zeal* for it. I truly wanted to make God active in my working life in ways I hadn't before. I'm not sure what brought this zeal on, but I do know that God has a way of waking us up to the realities of our Christian walk when we least expect it. I prayed more often during my shifts. Sometimes I'd listen to worship music with a single iPod earpiece as I worked. I would pray before the day began, covering the building and the people and the day with the Holy Spirit and the blood of the Lamb. And I did something else on a more frequent basis as well. I would begin the day by giving my desires to God. I handed over to him my desires for my future spouse, marriage and sexual intimacy (what I call the Three-Fold Longing). I did this regularly, sometimes multiple times a day to make sure I was truly giving it to God. I had plenty of success in this period. But the cycle had changed to accommodate my success.

On the days I failed in purity I began to see a daily pattern emerge. In the morning I'd wake up with a desire to fight lust for all it was worth. This was easy to do at work, since blatant temptation wasn't really around. I'm one of those people who can get very single-minded at work, meaning when I'm in the middle of a task

I drown out everything else. Work was lust-free most of the time. I would drive home to my grandma's place, watch Jeopardy or a movie with her, sometimes share a delicious meal. I'd go into my room to relax, check my email, watch another movie or some dumb YouTube video. I would write or tinker with screenplays on occasion. It was in the midst of all this down time that the sirens would sing to me. And when they called, they called loudly. All my zeal of the previous hours of the day would simply vanish. I'd see a single image of an attractive woman, and lust worked its hideous power. The defining war for my heart was back with a vengeance. In that period Satan would convince me to give in to some very specific lies: *You're a man with needs. Holding to these holy standards is too difficult, so go ahead and give in. And when you give in, give in big. You've been doing so well lately. Go ahead and reward yourself. You don't have to masturbate. Just take a look. You can lust without guilt. Go ahead and give in. God will forgive you anyway. He is merciful. He knows you're weak.*

Satan used all his accusatory half-truths to thoroughly convince me. And I fell for it. I, a young man who had tasted the freedom only Christ is capable of offering, who had been given so many powerful truths about sex and love and the heart of a woman. These seductions caused more shame and spiritual devastation. I *knew* I would give into my sin and just apologize later. I *knew* I could get off the hook guilt-free. Sometimes I'd fight the sirens for an hour before finally giving in. Other times I did nothing to fight back. But what so disturbed me about this new pattern was how quickly I found myself surrendering my strong beliefs for a worthless moment of solitary pleasure. My beliefs mattered deeply. I had my purity ring to remind me who I really needed to be pure for. I was deeply committed to those desires for purity and righteousness – for a while. This made the defeats more acute, more tangible, and more awful.

Thank God for Peter's request.

10

I was pretty fortunate to have Peter around in my journey through the slough of lust, because he and I struggled very much in tandem for most of it. Sometimes one of us would be enjoying a season of victory while the other would be suffering defeat. While we both would have preferred to not be struggling at all, it provided us with an amazing chance to act out in brotherly love and help each other get back on track. Iron sharpening iron. This was the other cycle that ran alongside the cycle of lust — a cycle of fellow suffering, transparency and repentance. There is nothing more encouraging than to realize there are other men struggling with the same things we do and that we are not alone in the fight. Satan loved to tell me that I was the only man in the world who struggled with purity. Peter was a great reminder that it was yet another lie.

When Peter went off to college we did not keep in touch as frequently as we should have. Sometimes a month would go by without contact, which was not good for either of us in our quest to overcome temptation. As a result of not being as present in each other's lives, we didn't know how we were doing, how our walks with the Lord were going, what kind of victories and defeats we were having (for those who are seeking accountability with other brothers, take my advice and never let it get to this point). We slipped into lust much easier in our own ways. After too much time had passed between seeing one another, we finally got together and talked about our struggles. We both knew the truth right away. For each of us, it had reached a point where something needed to be done.

Peter called me up again one day in some month of 2013 and proposed an idea: we begin to hold one another accountable. We had tried accountability years earlier without much success, and I was initially hesitant to go ahead with it. The accountability partner tactic is like most great ideas in the sense that it's easy to get excited about all the victory you're going to have and you become thrilled at the idea of having another guy standing right there with you in your trials. But all desires for accountability can quickly vanish when you are actually being tempted. The urge to call someone about it does not outmatch the urge to sin. When Peter said we should try it again, I didn't think it would yield any results. But after I thought about it more, the more I began to feel the Holy Spirit's pull. It didn't matter that we had failed with it previously. This was a good idea. This was something we should try again. Peter was aware of the reasons behind my disdain, but he persisted. Soon after, we decided to commit to it.

I can't remember who called first, probably Peter. He called me up, said he was in the thick of being tempted, would I please pray for him? I prayed for him and thanked him for having the courage to admit his struggle to me. It was after we were done talking that I realized what I had not been aware of with this issue of accountability – and why it hadn't worked in times past. When we had first tried to do it, we didn't tell each other about our temptation *in the moment*. Before, we would call one another *after* we had already given in, and then we would pray about it. That was all. The result of this formula was no results. But here, my brother-in-arms was telling me he was right in the middle of being tempted and that it needed to be dealt with right then and there. That was what we did from that point onward. For months we had amazing success over our flesh in this manner. Yes, we still failed sometimes. We still stumbled. We weren't always willing to call one another up the moment temptation hit. But an undeniable fact remained: We were on a steady stream of righteous victories.

However, the accountability didn't last for more than six months. We both let it fall by the wayside when life's distractions took us away from nurturing the state of our hearts. I didn't call him. He didn't call me. And so it faded away. The cycle was back with its devilish grin, waiting for me to let the door open. Which I did.

God then decided that 2013 would be the year to add to my library.

11

One day I recalled a quote I had read in John Eldredge's book *Walking With God*. In this book there rested one of those passages that jumps off the page and keeps your eyes pouring over it again and again: *What would your life be like if you were free of all that haunts you?*

When I first read the quote, I typed it out and taped it to the edge of my computer monitor. I did this to remind myself of the truth in case lust decided to come knocking. There were some other quotes I had taped up as well. One of them said "Give it to God," meaning the Three-Fold Longing. Another said "I am not my own. I belong to God." To my shame, I ignored these quotes most of the time. I would get on the computer without giving them a single glance. But now I re-read this particular quote and really *read* it, really paid attention to it and really pondered the answer to the question it asked.

What would my life be like if I never struggled with lust again? What if it was simply not a part of my life anymore? The question became a sort of mantra during that period, unable to leave my mind or my heart. I still lusted, sure. But the question remained. Out of curiosity I began looking online for any new books by Eldredge, and to my amazement I found one. It was called *The Utter Relief of Holiness*. The title was so captivating, so inviting, so reminiscent of what Christianity has the power to do in a person's life. Naturally, I bought the book and read it. As I read, I found a new spring of life welling within me.

Eldredge spoke of what it truly means to be holy. First off, I was amazed that this mysterious, mystical lifestyle called holiness was actually possible and available to struggling Christians like myself. It was one of those elements of Christianity I had heard of but never taken to heart, let alone believed could ever be attained. I was reminded that my faith is not a giant list of do's and dont's, but that it is freedom in Christ and freedom in knowing who you are in Christ. Christ commands us as his followers to be holy. Therefore, I reasoned, it must be possible to be holy. Being like Christ didn't suddenly feel so out-of-reach.

God revealed to me that one of the most pivotal aspects of the human heart was the issue of motives. In other words, everything we do, good or bad, has a motive behind it. Knowing this, I had to do something I had never done before. I had to pay close attention to my many life choices and the results of those choices. This whole period of spiritual discovery was also an amazing eye-opener into the character of Christ. I tried imagining what his motives might have been as he went about his ministry, what his thoughts were, and I wondered if I could ever have the same motives in my own decisions. In other words, if I could be holy. As I put these truths into practice in my life, I noticed that I was truly being honest with myself for the first time. I asked myself what my motives were in big and small decisions and began acting accordingly. My friendships grew in richness. My times of worship and prayer were some of the best I've ever experienced. It was intimacy with my Savior all over again. But it didn't stop there.

In another Amazon search, God led me to another book, specifically one dealing with godly manhood. It was called *God's Gift To Women* by Eric Ludy. What really struck me was the subtitle: *Discovering the Lost Greatness of Masculinity*. The lost greatness of masculinity. I was deeply impacted by those words. I saw a vision of manhood in that subtitle that I wanted to see made real. I thought about how decrepit manhood in the modern world has become. I remembered that God created men to be noble and honorable. I concluded that if the title was enough to fill me with righteous zeal, then the book must have great wisdom as well. So I picked it up.

As I read, God brought to me an aspect of the Christian walk that I had known before but never truly applied to my life: *manhood rises from mediocrity to greatness when it is one in body, mind and soul with its one and only King.* When a man knows who he is in Christ, who he serves and what his life's mission is all about – and thereby makes that his life – he is ushered into the company of the great. Great men don't care about what the world thinks of them or the King they serve. They only need approval from One. As I read these truths, I wondered how I could have neglected this for so long. This information wasn't new to me, but this time it was aimed at the heart. Before, it was just information. Now I understood that my devotion to Christ affected not just certain areas of my life, but every waking moment. I had a chance to make even the smallest of moments count for his glory.

After reading Ludy's book I was inspired to re-read *Jesus Freaks* by dc Talk and the Voice of the Martyrs. The book is a thorough collection of true stories about martyrs for Christianity throughout its history. These mighty people had this level of devotion and love for Christ that I was now rediscovering once again. After reading these books back-to-back, I was armed with the two-fold battle cry of holiness and loyal devotion. I was ready to live this stuff out. And I did. I dwelt on God all throughout the day in prayer and worship. I was growing into the man God wanted me to be. Life was great. For a time.

That hated companion was still clinging like a wound that would never heal.

It was late in 2013 that I allowed pornography into my story.

12

Up until this point in my journey, I didn't look at porn. Maybe it was because the movie lover in me couldn't get past the grimy cinematography and slipshod sound design. Maybe it was the cringe-inducing, eardrum-lancing dialogue (though last time I checked, men don't watch porn for its cinematic or artistic value). For whatever reason, I just couldn't bring myself to watch it. Something about watching people actually engage in real sex was uncomfortable and off-putting. It made me queasy in the way masturbation once did. I had also read a disturbing fact somewhere that came to mind whenever I thought about looking at porn. Medically speaking, it has been scientifically proven that pornography is more addictive than crack or heroin. Repeated use has the power to reconfigure the function of the human brain. This knowledge is a very scary reality. It only added to my desire to forever stay away from it.

I'm not sure when I first willingly watched porn, or what it actually was. All I know is that I found it when I wasn't looking for it. Like the health book ten years ago, it was an accidental awakening. I was in the middle of a lust session, looking at naked photos, when I noticed that a lot of those photography websites contained single images from various porn films. They showcased various positions, penetration, ejaculation, fellatio, things like that. Some of them advertised their sites with animated GIFs. I decided to slowly proceed with caution and hopefully find something soft-core. Tragically, I found it.

It started out small, but eventually I began to prefer watching videos of real sex over cinematic sex. They became just as appealing, if not more so, than the movie scenes. I never watched hardcore porn because I didn't find it arousing or even remotely appealing.

I knew enough to know that a lot of what happens in hardcore is borderline satanic, and I still have difficulty believing some men find it sexually arousing. As far as my own lust was concerned, I was after clean, simple and straightforward sex – the kind that the people in my favorite clips performed. I had individual favorites that I'd pull up when I decided to disregard my beliefs and not be the righteous man God wanted me to be. At that point I had developed favorites.

This persisted for the rest of the year and all through 2014. Over the course of the war God had instilled in me core ideals and truths about what it means to be a man of honor, sacrifice and holiness. And here I still remained, trapped in my cycle, clinging to a truth no man should ever know for himself: porn sure had some great-looking stuff. I still watched the movie scenes from time to time. Those never lost their appeal. I didn't want to admit to myself how good I had become at taking in every inch of a woman with my eyes. The addition of porn into the cycle brought a few other additions as well: deeper shame, deeper self-loathing, deeper belief that freedom from lust was impossible.

13

I suppose the next part of my journey is going to sound weird and irresponsible to a lot of readers. But if I can be open about a lifetime of lust, I can be open about the next step in my story. In August of 2014 God told me to begin living out of my car.

Actually, he had told me to live in my car months earlier. The reason it took me so long to actually begin doing it was for the understandable reason that I was scared to tell anyone. I knew a vast majority of my friends and family would tell me I hadn't actually heard from God, that it was dangerous, that my hygiene would go down the tubes, yada yada yada. Any sane person knows that living in a car goes against all notions of security. I was especially nervous about telling my grandma. She is famous in our family for her security measures. ADT, curtains over the windows, high fences, two front doors instead of one, gun by the bedside. I had lived with my grandma for three great years, and I was terrified about how she would react. So I decided to slowly tell my family, Peter, and a few other close friends individually. Their initial reactions were as expected, but when I told them that I believed God was in this, they began to understand.

My reasons for living out of my car were a combination of two different factors: a desire to live differently than everyone else, and because I felt God calling me away from my current life routine. I would wake up, go to work, come home, maybe hang out with my grandma, go in my room and relax to movies or Wikipedia articles or look for false comfort in the cycle, and I'd go to bed. That was my basic routine of life. It was a lifestyle of meaningless distraction. And I wanted out. I *needed* out. As always, God provided the right answer at the right time. I finally summoned the courage and told my grandma. She was surprisingly calm and understanding. One thing about my grandma that amazes me to this day is her willingness to not interfere. In spite of always wanting her loved ones close by, she wants her loved ones to have their own lives, and I was no exception. She wished me the best and told me she'd be praying for me. When August rolled around I began moving my stuff out and taking it back to my old room in my parents' place. I took only what I needed with me in the car, and thus began a new way of life.

As one can easily imagine, it was initially awkward at first. My first couple nights were very much sleep-deprived, as I was constantly waiting for the cops to knock on my window and haul me to the nearest jail cell. During the first week I didn't have a gym membership, so I was cleansing myself at various park or gas station restrooms (which works a lot better than you may think). I would go to McDonald's or Barnes & Noble and work on various writing projects, something I loved to do and rarely did back at my grandma's place. I reclaimed my long-lost status as an avid reader. I can remember reading *The Pillars of the Earth* under an Albertsons parking lot light for three weeks, or hastily trying to finish the next chapter of *The Bonfire of the Vanities* and *Blood Meridian* before I lost the light. I was loving the outlaw feel of living so uniquely and feeling like I was living the way I wanted to live. And I was loving what God was doing in my life.

As I was listening to his voice and seeking his guidance on what this time in the car was all about, God met me. I prayed for a few of my friends at work in the middle of work hours, which was not something I had the courage to do a year earlier. I met a homeless man outside a coffee shop, had a good conversation and ended up giving him eighty dollars. Giving to the homeless wasn't something I'd ever done before. A couple times I was all hunkered down for the night, only to receive a call from a friend who needed prayer and encouragement, thereby forcing me to put my night of solitary comfort on hold. I don't know anyone who likes having their agenda interfered with, least of all me. One night I couldn't sleep at all because of the legendary Seattle rain pounding on my car roof. One

35

time I asked the Lord to take the rain away so I could sleep, which he did in fifteen minutes.

As I sought the Lord's guidance, I discovered what this time was really about. The main theme of my time in the car was *obedience*. I was learning to obey God in living like this and responding to the opportunities to obey him at any given time. Living in my car was not the key to my spiritual success. It was through my obedience of doing it that God was revealing things to me and getting to the heart of certain issues in my life. And I had victories over lust. Sometimes.

There were nights where I stayed with my folks or my grandma's, either because I had to be in the area the following day or my folks were out of town and needed a housesitter or because it was so rainy I couldn't sleep. Either way, when I went back to both houses at various times, lust was waiting there for me. In my car I was very focused on God and I had the zeal to resist the sirens. Due to limited Internet access and not wanting to be seen, I couldn't just get online and look up porn or movie scenes. But at both homes, I let my guard down and it was back to the cycle all over again.

There was one Sunday morning I can specifically recall. I had stayed over at my grandma's and was heading out. The night before I had given in to lust. I was deeply ashamed because I had been so successful for about two weeks while living in my car. Two weeks was a pretty great run for someone as willing to please the flesh as me. I was driving to church and before me was an amazing sunrise. Washington has gorgeous sunrises and sunsets, but this one was truly special. It was special because it came with words from the Holy Spirit. In the midst of my repentance he spoke three words: "I forgive you." In all my history of lusting and affairs of the heart and stealing with my eyes, I rarely *felt* forgiven after repenting. But I did that morning. I could literally feel my spirit being cleansed. My King's forgiveness had never felt so real. It was as real as the sunrise before me. I practically cried my way to church.

14

It was about December 15th that I temporarily moved back into my folks' house. I had still been regularly living out of my car, despite the nights getting as cold as 25 degrees. But since Christmas was coming I wanted to go home and be with family. I ended up staying late into January, even though the holidays were over and the weather was warmer. I could have gone back to my car many times. I *should* have gone back. But I wasn't being obedient. I wasn't holding onto the times God had come through on my behalf in the past months. As a result, that most hated companion had firmly rooted itself back into my life. I was lusting every two or three days at most, either going back to the movie scenes, porn or old memories, all of which culminated in masturbation. Never did I look at an image or watch a scene without masturbating. I found that mornings were extremely difficult. Mornings were always difficult during the war, especially right as I was waking up. I'd be awake and half-asleep, my guard mostly down, and the sexy images, sounds and sensations would return to my mind. Sometimes I'd masturbate in bed barely minutes into my day.

I discovered one thing around this time about lust that I had never caught before. Whenever I allowed myself to give in, it seemed to throw everything else in my life out of tune. I'd be "off" spiritually, mentally and emotionally. Driving to work while listening to beautiful music wasn't nearly as rich. I didn't see or acknowledge beauty as often. My evenings were vapid. Life was simply not as good after I had lusted, even after I had repented. By this time Satan had injected a lie into my heart that I honestly believed, because it seemed completely true: "This sin will always be in your life." I had a week or a month of awesome, God-honoring victory, but sooner or later lust would come back like Hurricane Katrina. I'd give in eventually.

I felt doomed to a lifetime of going back to square one. This was a pattern I had seen before. After a solid span of time in which God helped me conquer lust, my guard would come down. I'd start out with the same perfectly honorable thoughts. *I can't wait to get married. I can't wait to see my wife first thing in the morning. I can't wait to have sex with her.* Images. Lust. Masturbation. Like clockwork. But hey, at least I had grace and forgiveness to fall back on. Even though this sin would always be in my life, I knew God would be there. I should have had hope. Instead I had despair about as deep as the ocean's abyssal plain. My belief that freedom from lust was actually possible was diminishing. No matter where I turned, it was there, lying in wait to devour me whole. One escapade of lust corrupted a whole week of victory in my eyes. I had come to believe it was true. This sin would always be in my life.

Around mid-January of 2015 I was preparing to resume living in my car.

I was staying at my grandma's.

I gave in to lust that night.

I came across a quote online.

It was the beginning of my Second Great Awakening.

15

There wasn't anything particularly different about that day or night. It was just another day. My grandma was in bed and I was still awake. I love staying up late. I've been a night owl for a good portion of my life. I was at my computer, browsing and reading articles and listening to music. Then it came. Lust was back. I must have seen some random scintillating picture. You can probably fill in the blanks as to what happened next. Within minutes I pulled up one of my porn favorites, and soon I had fully given in. I felt the shame, rage and frustration, feelings that had stalked me like a demon gang since the beginning of the war I had waged since I was thirteen. This time I was pretty upset. Sometimes those feelings were far worse than other times. This night was particularly awful. I gave myself absolutely no slack. It's fair to say that after lusting that night I *hated* myself.

I went into my grandma's living room to repent to God. Her computer sits on a desk near the recliners, and I decided to log on. I typed in the search bar a single word: *porn*. I saw a list of recent searches that contained that word, and the one at the very top caught my eye. I could tell that it was some kind of quote, so I gave it a click. The web page came onscreen, and I saw the quote in its entirety: "I'm not interested in a world where men really want to watch porn but resist because they've been shamed; I'm interested in a world where men are raised from birth with such an unshakable understanding of women as living human beings that they are incapable of being aroused by their exploitation."

You could have heard the chord in my soul being struck had you been listening for it. It was the last sentence in particular that really haunted me. A world of men incapable of being aroused by porn because of the reality of what it is and what it does to women. I repented on the spot, the kind of repenting that is honest and comes out of sincere sorrow directly from the heart. Immediately after I asked myself a question: Was such a world even possible? By the end of it, as I felt the cleansing of the Holy Spirit, I was reminded of something ironic that had occurred on occasion during the war.

There would be times where I would give in and repent with the same honesty that I had just done, which would then be followed by a time of deep and intimate prayer and worship to my God. In other words, some of my greatest times of intimacy with God came directly after my escapades of lust. This was one of those times. I went to bed that night feeling God's presence and the sense of being truly forgiven. Forgiven and haunted by the quote I had read. I found out later that the quote was actually an excerpt from an online conversation my cousin had just recently been a part of on my grandma's computer a few days prior to that night. Looking back, it seems as though God had set up the whole encounter all along.

The next thing the Lord did in my life is the sort of thing that makes me wish books could come with rousing cinematic soundtracks. Picture these movie scenes:

Scottish warriors charging the fields of Bannockburn to claim their freedom at the end of *Braveheart*.

The One Ring being tossed into the fires of Mount Doom at the climax of *The Lord of the Rings*.

The end of the film *In the Name of the Father*, in which a wrongfully imprisoned man is released after fifteen years. The guards try to hold him back after he is pronounced innocent, and he says right to their faces, "I'm a free man and I'm going out the front door."

These are illustrations of what God did next.

And he did it with another quote.

The following week was lust-free. I could not get that quote out of my mind and the question it raised. After all that I had endured and all the sin I had allowed into my life, after all the affairs of the heart I had committed, was it truly possible to be free from lust in a world where lust runs amok like a serial killer who always evades capture? As I pondered all these things in my mind and soul, God reminded me of an article I had read about a year before. It was titled "Lust as I See It - Part I," by Christian counselor and writer Sam Jolman. When I read it the previous year, I had been touched by his story and insight. I even wrote the final sentence of the article down and put it in my wallet. But now I realize I only did that to make myself feel good for believing something that was right. Ultimately, it was real for Jolman, but it wasn't real for me. Remember, I had come to believe lust would be a part of my life forever. I had firmly made that agreement and had held onto it for years. When I re-read the article, it was like I was receiving the truth for the first time.

In the article, Jolman shared, in his words, "a vulnerable part of my story." He confessed two things: he used to be addicted to pornography, and his wife was an artist who loved drawing nude figures. He goes on: "You'd think I would have a major problem on my hands, that my wife's [artistic] love and my idolatry would mix like oil and water. Or better put, gasoline and a match, inflaming the lust of my heart. In reality, my wife's art has been balm to my broken sexuality, helping to heal me from the destructive effects of my porn use."

As impactful as these words were, they also confused me. I didn't understand how something like this aesthetic cure he was talking about was possible. I kept aligning his story with mine and not seeing how anything remotely like this could be done in my own life. But as I read on, I was rediscovering a specific truth – not about sex, not about porn, not about marriage, not about idolatry. It was a truth about Eve herself. It was about Woman. I read the final sentence, the one I had in my wallet but not in my heart: "Can you conceive of a world in which the beauty of women only all the time moved men to worship their God?"

41

I had originally just sat down to read an old article.

I never expected to leave with the keys to my freedom.

I opened the door that had been calling to be opened for twelve years.

I decided to go through.

PART II: What I Learned

– Folk in those stories had lots of chances of turning back, only they didn't. They kept going. Because they were holding on to something.
– What are we holding on to, Sam?
(Sam stands Frodo up and looks him straight in the eye)
– That there's some good in this world, Mr. Frodo. And it's worth fighting for.

– The Lord of the Rings: The Two Towers

I walk this earth a free man.

Sure, I still choose to sin. I stumble. I am still learning the ways of the heart and how I can trust God wholeheartedly in all areas of my life. I am learning how to confront my fears. I am still on life's journey. But the sin of lust is no longer the defining struggle of my life. It still tries to seduce me, to tell me that I am not really free, beckoning me to come back. My situation is similar to the character Neo in *The Matrix* trilogy. After being trapped since birth by the illusion and imprisonment of the Matrix, Neo is freed. He is given his true name, his true identity, and ultimately, his purpose. Throughout his quest he sometimes encounters the evil and corrupted Agent Smith. Every time these two meet, Smith addresses Neo by the name he had while in control of the Matrix: Mr. Anderson. He tries to convince him that he has no purpose, no destiny, and ultimately, that he is not really free.

This freedom you think you have is an illusion. These are Satan's words, and he has used them since his fall from Paradise to deceive God's people. But God has taken hold of the pen and rewritten my story. He continually reminds me that through Christ's redeeming work I have authority over this sin, and by his power in me I can send lust limping back to the pit of hell. The strength of the one I serve is greater than the strength of the one who steals, kills and destroys all that he made to be good, pure and innocent. It is not my strength, but *his* strength that gives me any chance of conquering the schemes of the evil one. This is the truth I walk in even as I write these words. When I read the final sentence of Jolman's article that second time in early 2015, all that I knew to be true about sexual purity and the female body ceased to be head knowledge and instead became heart knowledge. I took his question as a holy challenge. I took it on because I knew in my heart that it was the life I wanted – that it was a life that was possible.

The Word says in Ephesians 5:3 that "among you there must not be even a hint of sexual immorality, or of any kind of impurity." A very high, noble command. But, like the roaring lion of I Peter 5:8, lust lurks everywhere in our world today. During the war,

Satan convinced me that this command to be sexually pure was an impossible, even unrealistic command to keep. *Scott, this is how the real world works. Everyone else is doing it and having a great time. Lust is safe and comfortable. It doesn't really hurt anyone, you least of all. No one will condemn you for it because that's how men are these days. Face the truth: Nobody else wants what you want. Why are you wasting your time?* Like a furnace whose fire refuses to run dry, Satan has projected these lies over and over again. But I know the truth, and the truth is that no matter how powerful the kingdom of darkness is, it will not overcome the King of Kings.

Now that you've read my story, I want to spend the rest of our time together telling you, my fellow brothers in Christ, how you can conquer the scourge of lust in your own lives by applying and living out the knowledge and the truth God brought to me. I highly encourage any women reading this to continue on as well. When I sat down to write my story I wanted women to read it just as much as men. I want you, my sisters in the Lord, to see firsthand how deeply lust affects men in our fallen world, what their struggle looks like, and ultimately, how you can help men win the fight. I want you to see how vast and deep your beauty truly is and how it has the power to draw us into authentic worship and further strengthen our relationships with God. This is how it is with me. My romance with Christ has only grown deeper and continues to strengthen to this day, and one of the primary ways in which this happens is a result of all he continually reveals to me through the gift of feminine beauty.

I don't know your stories, men. I don't know how much damage has been done in your lives and relationships because of lust. Some of you may be in the boat I was once in: struggling, but keeping other women from physical and spiritual harm. Some of you may be deeply addicted to pornography without hope of escape. Some of you may be divorced, had children out of wedlock, or have gone through the pain of abortion. Maybe you currently have girlfriends or have had many girlfriends. I don't know. But I do know this: Jesus came to set us free, and that freedom is available to all who truly desire it. By his hand you can overcome this sin so wholly and so completely that you can forget what is behind, press on toward the goal with your brothers-in-arms and ring out the battle cry of victory that was won for you and me on the cross of Calvary.

Let's continue on together.

The Heart

Above all else, guard your heart, for it is the wellspring of life.
— Proverbs 4:21

I love this verse. To me, it is one of the most useful, helpful, and insightful verses in all of Scripture. Much of the problems we have and face in this life can be solved by doing exactly what this verse instructs. Most of those problems would not even exist if we simply did what it said. When talking about lust, this verse is all the more urgent and necessary. The church has spent a fair amount of time and resources giving its men advice on what to do to avoid impurity of the body, the mind and the spirit. I have nothing against the church's wisdom in this area. I have acted on it many times in my life and I still do. Look at the world around you and it is obvious why the church has so many resources to help godly men remain pure.

But I believe something is missing. I believe men have only been given one half of the solution to the problem of dealing with lust effectively, and this mostly consists of what *not* to do. I recall attending a men's conference years ago, and there was a program for men struggling with pornography. At the end we were given a pamphlet that had verses about purity and practical steps to avoid any traps that could lead us back to porn. The verses were great. The advice was good. But there was nothing beyond, "Don't do this, stay away from that." Somehow, it didn't feel complete. If this is truly all it takes to remain pure, why do so many of God's men still struggle with lust?

As amazing as it is, when I look back over my war, I don't recall ever discovering what lust actually is in reality. All I remember reading or hearing was what I and my fellow brothers in the Lord already knew. "Lust is bad. Lust is a perversion. Lust is wicked. Lust is evil." As true as this is, it ultimately offers nothing helpful in solving the problem. Hearing this time and time again is similar to a mechanic telling a desperate person their car engine is dead . . . and then walking away. Had I known what lust really is, the war for my soul could have been shortened or maybe eliminated altogether.

What the church needs to start telling its men is that lust is first and foremost an issue of the *heart*. One of the most widely-believed misconceptions is that the mind and the eyes are where lust comes from. It seems true on the surface. The mind and the eyes have power we cannot ignore. But in reality, both of these are instruments that serve a far greater force. Our thoughts and our actions are the result of what comes out of the heart. That includes how we look at, think about, and behave towards women. We may lustfully gaze at clothed or unclothed women with our physical eyes. Our minds may create fantasies of sexual immorality with the women we see. But the only reason these things happen in the first place is because of what is stirring in our hearts. Jesus himself said it best:

> "For *out of the heart* come evil thoughts, murder, adultery, sexual immorality, theft, false testimony, slander. These are what make a man 'unclean'" (Matthew 15:19-20, emphasis added). . .

I recently read a heartbreaking article about a boy and girl caught up in a sexting scandal a few years ago. It began like many sexting scandals do: the boy repeatedly asked this girl to send photos of herself to his phone. He made it clear that she did not have to be fully naked. All she had to do was wear sexy lingerie and blur her face out of the image so she could not be identified. Of course, he didn't ask her to do any of this upon first getting to know her (no man wants to instantly come off to a lady as a night-crawling, porn-watching, masturbatory sociopath). He was a charming guy. He had a way with sweet talk. By the time he made his request they had become friends. He used his charisma to convince the girl that she had nothing to worry about. He told her that he planned to delete the pictures after he'd seen them. She eventually sent him photos. It was not because she was caving into his demands. She wasn't tired of being pestered. She sent them because she liked the attention. She came to trust him. She felt safe with this boy. Everything he promised was completely convincing.

Tragically, he lied about deleting the images. Through a series of events the photos spread around the kids' school from one phone to another. When both of them were eventually caught, the consequences of what they had done almost ruined their lives and the lives of those closest to them.

This story – like stories about bullying and school shootings – raises many questions. One cannot help but ask what could have been done to prevent this whole debacle, which in turn makes us wonder what we can be doing right now to keep things like this from ever happening again. Some may say, "The parents should have been more involved." "The kids should not have been allowed to have smartphones." "Tighter classroom control." "More intervention from the school." "The boy should have seen a psychologist." On and on it goes. But none of these seemingly legitimate solutions is the correct answer. The real answer is not so obvious. It ultimately has nothing to do with what other people have the power to control. The answer lies with the condition of the boy's heart. If the boy had not acted on the wickedness within him – if he had chosen to be honest with himself and acknowledged that what he wanted to do was evil – none of the ensuing devastation would have happened. Not a single life would have been destroyed had he identified the lust in his heart and said, "No." This is not just one boy, either. This is you. This is me. This is all of us. It is that simple, that difficult, and that enormous.

A man worships God from his heart. A man engages in activities and hobbies that he takes pleasure in because his desires to do so come from his heart. A man listens to specific types of music because it is from the heart that the desire to listen to that music comes. A man looks at pornography because of the condition of his heart. A man admires artwork portraying the naked female body because of the condition of his heart. Like the trail of crumbs from *Hansel and Gretel*, everything we do or think and why it all happens ultimately leads back to the heart. Most of the time, we are unaware of this. We too easily dismiss our actions without really thinking about why we do them at all. We dismiss our thoughts as nothing more than thoughts.

Sometimes a man who lusts after a woman convinces himself that he is at the mercy of his heart, that he has no control over what he's doing because "the heart wants what it wants, so therefore my actions are justified." A man who makes such an excuse is a man who does not know his heart very well. The verse above does not say, "Above all else, *follow* your heart." Jeremiah 17:9 reminds us that "the heart is deceitful above all things." If our hearts are not in the hands of Christ, how much more so are those hearts capable of being deceived! (Ecclesiastes 11:9 is the only place in the Bible I recall that says to follow your heart, and the end of the passage is quite insightful: "Follow the ways of your heart and whatever your eyes see, but know that for all these things God will bring you to judgment").

Here is a scenario that has happened to me and to many other men. A man is on the computer, and he suddenly finds this desire to look at porn come over him like a hideous cloud of raving no-see-ums. Maybe this desire is born out of memories of a previous encounter. Perhaps he wants to add some new additions to his porn dungeon. It could be that he has no wish to fulfill the desire at all. In this situation one of two things can happen. The man can shut the computer off and run away, or he can give in to temptation. As he faces the screen, the man does an uncommon thing and actually asks himself why he's doing what he's doing.

He resists temptation. He asks why. He says, "Because this is an evil sin against God, women and myself." Now here is the reverse. He gives in to temptation. He asks himself why. He says, "Because I wanted the pleasure porn brings me." Notice what he does *not* do. He does not waste time by blaming outside forces, pointing fingers, claiming he is "only human," or making a thousand other lame excuses to justify his actions. Our man chooses to be honest. He is honest because he is aware that it is because of the condition of his heart – his wellspring of life – that he is doing what he's doing. This is not a complex scenario, and the two outcomes are not complex. But because it is an issue of the heart, the implications and the results have the power to alter the course of the man's life.

Our hearts contain evil desires. The Bible reminds us of this over and over again. Story after story illustrates men and women choosing to follow death instead of life. The message runs through the Bible from beginning to end: without God as our master and savior, the evil in our hearts can lead us further away from what we need to be free. When it comes to deceiving a man struggling with lust, Satan uses this knowledge to his advantage. In the times where we give in to temptation, our enemy tries to convince us that our hearts themselves are evil. It is a brilliant tactic because that accusation is incredibly convincing. But this is not the case. Paul famously explains this issue in Romans 7. It is a passage that I encountered quite a bit when hearing talks or reading books about sexual purity. Looking at it closer reveals much more:

> We know that the law is spiritual; but I am unspiritual, sold as a slave to sin. I do not understand what I do. For what I want to do I do not do, but what I hate I do. And if I do what I do not want to do, I agree that the law is good. As it is, it is no longer I myself who do it, but it is sin living in me. For I know that good itself does not dwell in me, that is, in my sinful nature. For I have the desire to do what is good, but I cannot carry it out. For I do not do the good I want to do, but the evil I do not want to do—this I keep on doing. Now if I do what I do not want to do, it is no longer I who do it, but it is sin living in me that does it.
> So I find this law at work: Although I want to do good, evil is right there with me. For in my inner being I delight in God's law; but

I see another law at work in me, waging war against the law of my mind and making me a prisoner of the law of sin at work within me. What a wretched man I am! Who will rescue me from this body that is subject to death? Thanks be to God, who delivers me through Jesus Christ our Lord!

So then, I myself in my mind am a slave to God's law, but in my sinful nature a slave to the law of sin (14-25).

Do you see what Paul is saying? *This is not me, but the sin living in me that does these things. Though sin lives in me, it does not define me. I love God with all my heart. I want to do good. That is my true self. But evil is right there, working to imprison me. Thank you that Jesus delivers me from this!* The great paradox of our fallen humanity is this: We can love Jesus and be holy and still sin. But the freedom-giving news is that the law of sin is no longer what is true about us. It no longer has the claim it once had over our lives because Jesus set us free from that law.

Even though we walk this earth as free men in Christ, sin will happen, and it will happen until God takes us home. As long as we live on this broken earth, we will never fully escape the curse of the Fall. But a life in devotion to the sinful nature is something we can choose to leave behind. Christ is telling us to leave that life because it is not who we are anymore. Jesus was so insightful when he claimed he was not bringing peace, but a sword. He did not come to give us some nice-sounding sermons that we would forget in half an hour. *He did not come to leave us where we are.* No. He came to declare war on the ways of the sinful nature that hold the world enslaved. When we made the decision to choose Christ instead of the world, he broke that sinful life within us.

Jesus died on the cross for our sins and rose victorious on the third day. He died to set us free from the old covenant of the law to place us under the law of grace. This law of grace is something that we must never forget or misinterpret. We need to remind ourselves of the law of grace every day until it becomes our way of life, for it is by his grace that we are freed from the law of sin and death, which held onto us before we accepted Christ into our hearts. The ways of the sinful nature have been permanently cleansed by the death and resurrection of our Savior. The rest of the Bible then tells us not to use the grace of the cross as a means to justify sin. Instead, we are told to put off the ways of the sinful nature because we are not under that law anymore. To keep living under that law is to remain a slave. It is for freedom that Christ came to set us free (Galatians 5:1), and whoever the Son has set free, that person is free indeed (John 8:36). These next passages of Scripture reveal what happens to our hearts and our lives when we choose to follow Christ instead of the world:

> What shall we say, then? Shall we go on sinning so that grace may increase? By no means! We died to sin; how can we live in it any longer? (Romans 6:1-4).

> In the same way, count yourselves dead to sin but alive to God in Christ Jesus. Therefore do not let sin reign in your mortal body so that you obey its evil desires. . . for sin shall no longer be your master, because you are not under the law, but under grace (Romans 11:14).

> But now that you have been set free from sin and have become slaves of God, the benefit you reap leads to holiness, and the result is eternal life. For the wages of sin is death, but the gift of God is eternal life in Christ Jesus our Lord (Romans 6:19-23).

> Those who live according to the flesh have their minds set on what the flesh desires; but those who live in accordance with the Spirit have their minds set on what the Spirit desires (Romans 8:5).

> Rather, clothe yourselves with the Lord Jesus Christ, and do not think about how to gratify the desires of the sinful nature (Romans 13:14).

This is such awesome news! It makes me want to jump up and shout for joy. What we men need to realize is that the freedom we so long to experience from lust has been there the whole time. When we gave our hearts to Christ, the deliverance from lust through the freedom of grace became ours forever. He took our sin and condemnation and disarmed its power over our lives and souls by his glorious triumph. Though we still stumble by choosing to sin, we can still choose freedom because that is what Jesus came to give us (Galatians 5:1).

When I finished this book, I did not expect to ever give in to lust again. For at least a year-and-a-half this was true. I did not give into it, nor did I allow it to fester in my mind. But I began to have times of weakness in which I chose lust over freedom. I became afraid after these moments of stumbling. I would hear many voices convincing me that it was only a matter of time before this freedom-from-lust facade was exposed. *Oh no! The cycle is back! I'm doomed! I thought I was free from this forever!* These moments of weakness scared me to death. But as loud as those voices were, I found myself listening to a different voice. The words of Scripture reminded me of what was really going on: I stumbled, yet I was free. And from then on my prayers began to change. Instead of begging God to destroy the cycle before it began again after all he had done to set me free, I began to praise God for the freedom that his son won for me on the old rugged cross, the freedom I could choose to walk in every day.

This change in the way I prayed and what I prayed convinced me that this is what God's men need to do in such moments of defeat. Instead of crying out to God to set us free, we need to cry out shouts of thanksgiving that we are *already* free. The moment we made the decision to let Christ be the Lord of our lives, the chains came off forever. If we would only stop putting those chains back on, we could see just how vast the promise of his grace truly is. Thinking about all of this reminds me of a line from *Saving Private Ryan*, one of my favorite films of all time. After the final battle, Capt. John Miller tells Ryan with his dying breath, "Earn this." At the end of the film, an elderly Ryan looks at his wife and pleads with her to tell him that he was a good man. You get the feeling just by looking at his eyes that he has spent his entire life with the gnawing certainty that he has not earned the sacrifice those men made for him in the war.

I wonder how many Christians feel this way about what Christ accomplished for us. "You have to earn it" is the underlying mantra of all other religions, and many fellow brothers and sisters in Christ believe the same about our salvation. We somehow cannot accept the fact that Jesus used the cross to tell us something: "I've earned it for you. Stop trying." I learned after my war that true and lasting freedom from lust is not something I have to earn. Satan convinced me many times over that in order to be free from lust, *I* had to be the one to do it. And because I was an evil man, I could never be free. Thanks be to God forever that Jesus did it for me! When we choose this freedom and this forgiveness by giving our hearts to Christ, he then tells us the same thing he told the adulteress in John 8:11: "Go and leave your life of sin."

Men, we need to start seeing lust for what it truly is: a war for our hearts. Satan wants our hearts because the heart is everything. If sin perverts the wellspring, it perverts everything that flows from it. When we look at our actions and sinful choices, we begin to realize that *we* are the ones who give Satan any power he has in our lives. We do this by believing in and acting on his lies, of which the Word calls him "the father" (John 8:44). When I gave in to lust, I was exchanging truth for deception. One of the biggest lies I believed was that after giving into lust I was somehow going back to Square One with God, that all the times I resisted temptation in the past did not matter because I gave in to lust and I now had to start earning his favor all over again. How beautiful to know that this is an absolute lie. How wonderful to know that his favor is not earned, but freely given.

The more we cling to sin, the more easily we will believe that sin is what defines us. Satan says we are still the same men we were when we were shackled in bondage. God says we are free, and what God says about you is the truth. When we see our hearts with the eyes of the God we serve, we begin to realize that we are not evil men, but deceived men. Our hearts are good. The sin living in us and our choice to follow that sin is what is to blame. Sin is a choice. So is righteousness. Once we choose to walk this path, we will begin to see the enemy's lies and fight back with what God says about us. Lust tells us we are evil. God says we are the royal priesthood in whom his Spirit dwells.

I love how the Word refers to the act of taking in its wisdom as "writing on the tablet of our heart." It implies that once it's there, it's there to stay. The engraving on the stone may be covered with dirt and moss, but we can choose to clean it off. Though the writing may be covered, that writing is not going anywhere. It is there to stay.

Let us start writing the truth on the tablets of our hearts.

Let us make sure that it stays.

Not for a little while. Forever.

CHRIST

One thing I ask from the Lord, this is what I seek:
that I may dwell in the house of the Lord all the days of my life,
to gaze on the beauty of the Lord
and to seek him in his temple.

— Psalm 27:4

When I look back over the events of the war, I see clearly that I am only free because of one thing: *relationship*. When you think about it, relationship is the absolute bedrock of Christianity. We can see this in the life of Jesus. He was constantly in relationship with his disciples, his family and those he ministered to. Though we do not see many examples in Scripture, he had his moments of solitude. After John the Baptist was beheaded, Jesus went off to a solitary place. He was stricken deeply with grief at the death of his close friend. I think it's fair, even realistic, to say that Jesus *needed* solitude. I have never experienced grief on this scale, but when I am grieving in any way, the last thing I want to do is help people in need. Quite ironic, then, that the crowds of needy people find him. How does Jesus respond? Directly following this period of intense sorrow Jesus performs one of the most famous miracles in the Bible. He miraculously feeds five thousand people. He has compassion on them. He relates to them. He offers himself in the heat of incredibly painful circumstances.

Another great scene is Jesus's temptation. After a period of forty days of fasting in the wilderness and enduring intense warfare against Satan – all on his own – angels come to minister to him. Like so many gems in the Bible, we often pass this section over with a nod and a glance without really thinking about the truth it holds. Psychologically, spiritually and emotionally, Jesus has been through

58

the fire. The angels don't come just to attend him. They come to be in *community* with him. They come to offer not just food, but their very presence. These brief episodes tell us something very important: Life and holiness cannot be had apart from relationship.

Men like to be alone. I have yet to meet a man who is constantly looking for ways to be around other people. In looking at my own life and the lives of men I know, I have come to see that men draw a lot of strength from being off by themselves. Solitude is a fundamental characteristic of masculinity that is not as prevalent among women. Of course, men love coming together for plain old fun or deep fellowship as much as anyone. But there is a tremendous, life-giving serenity that comes with solitude that does not and cannot happen in community. Just look across the stories men love, and you will find countless examples of heroic loners. Lone wolves are often held up in popular culture as definitive examples of the masculine ideal. But things get dangerous for a man when that life-giving solitude becomes his way of life. When this happens, life eventually gives way to death. Many of those heroic loners often discover at a tremendous cost how destructive their solitary lives truly are.

When we spend most of our lives with no one but ourselves and all our sins, wounds and demons for company, we are ignoring the very community that Christ made an absolute priority.

Peter, my closest ally and brother in Christ, once told me that while he was living in his college dorm, he became so lonely that he thought he was going insane because he found himself talking to the plant on his windowsill. I never forgot his words because it was such a graphic picture of the truth. Extreme as it may seem, this is what a life of solitude really looks like. Eventually, whether we will acknowledge it or not, solitude turns into our own private hell. Loneliness will happen. It cannot be avoided. So in our loneliness we inevitably turn to something that does not make us feel lonely, something that requires little to nothing of us and makes us feel good. Many times, we turn to lust.

Lust is the classic false comfort. It calls to us in our solitude, and we answer. We feel good for a short while, then the feelings of loneliness and isolation come back like a rogue wave and suddenly it is all we know. We start to believe the lies all over again. One of the worst things about this issue of solitude is that while we are focused on easing our pain with sin, we don't offer anything back to anyone. We do not offer because Satan tells us the lie that *we have nothing to offer.* What God has been trying to tell us the entire time is the exact opposite. Every man has strength to offer. Every man has relationship to offer. Every man is called to offer. Look again at our Savior. Practically every story in the Gospel illustrates this: *I am the light of the world. I have something you need, and I am going to give it to you.* What he had that the world needed was himself. Jesus was all about offering *himself.* I know this to be true. He has been offering himself to me my whole life.

One of the great ways God gets to my heart is through worship music. Some of the richest times in my spiritual life were often timed with the discovery of new praise music. I would get a new album and worship my heart out for a period of time. But after that time, I didn't always have that instant connection with God through the music. Not every worship time involved tears of joy. I was not always engaged in body, mind and heart when I sang. Initially, I was bothered by this. It bothered me because it seemed like if I couldn't get to that place every time I worshiped, something wasn't right. But as I grew and matured in my relationship with Christ, I learned that it doesn't always have to be that way. It *shouldn't* always be that way.

Most of the time, our relationship is alive and tangible to me, but there are times when I do not feel our usual closeness. Sometimes he feels quite far away. There are times of oneness and distance, intimacy and separation. How does one make sense of this? If I were to view this back-and-forth dynamic in purely human terms, it seems quite problematic, as if God sometimes chooses not to engage with me because he doesn't feel like it or his schedule is too full or not right now, maybe later. But I've learned over the years that I cannot place a relationship with God in a human box. God does not relate to me or pursue me like one of my fellow flawed, fallen and imperfect human beings that I live with in the same world. Comparing God's way of loving to a fellow human's way of loving simply doesn't work.

The Word assures us that he is the same yesterday, today and forever (Hebrews 13:8). He is always waiting for me to come back to our sacred intimacy. He will never use the words, "Scott, I am far too busy." Whether I am aware of it or not, he is always pursuing me. When I am not close to Jesus, it is because I am not choosing to be close. Like a marriage that lacks passion, I am not doing what I could be doing to cultivate intimacy. Though he is always with me, intimacy with Christ does not always come easy. It does not always come romantically. Sometimes the only way it can grow is through trial and tribulation or a period of suffering. Like my human relationships, I have days where I want to remain in my own world and not make any effort at relational oneness. Relationships take work, and I don't always want to work. The poisonous nature of lust is that it takes no work at all. Lust is despicably easy. It requires nothing of us. It promises intimacy, but, as we know full well, proves to be nothing but a fraud. Lust is nothing if not false intimacy. When I lusted, I chased after whatever gave me that feeling of intimacy without my having to give any in return. I sought intimacy with something other than God. Look how well it turned out.

The most important thing I learned is that a man cannot know lasting freedom from lust without a relationship with Jesus Christ. He might as well jump out of a plane and refuse to pull his parachute in the hope of surviving the fall. Freedom rests in Christ alone, and our savior wants his men to remove anything and everything that could potentially hinder and usurp that sacred relationship. As I write this I'm reminded of another powerful line from *Saving Private Ryan*. Capt. Miller is conversing with his soldiers after one of his men is killed, and he tells them with a tangible weariness, "I just know that with every man I kill the farther away from home I feel." How true this is about what sin does to us. When I face my own sin, that's how it feels. Whenever I lusted God felt less real, less available, less present.

But the wonderful news is that Christianity is not built upon what we feel about it. Human feeling is not the foundation of our faith. Whether we *feel* if God is close or not does not change the truth that he *is* close. Relationship with him is real and available, brothers. It is. If you seek him with all your heart, you will find him. It can be yours.

> You will find me when you seek me with all your heart.
> — Jeremiah 29:13

Make this heavenly relationship your primary reason for seeking freedom from lust.

It is difficult. It requires a lot of you. And there is nothing more worth fighting for.

Your desire for purity should not be about making women more attracted to you.

Your desire should be to cultivate a lifetime of sacred intimacy with your Savior.

As all men have something to offer the world, so you too have something to offer God.

Act on your desire for purity with a heart of giving back to Christ what he has given to you.

Believe me when I say he will woo you in lavish, abundant measure.

Female Relationship

One of my closest friends wrote me a letter recently. It was to commemorate our one-year friendship anniversary. She is an anniversary-loving individual, not to mention phenomenally good at keeping track of birthdays and special dates. We joke that she has to remind me of planned outings and get-togethers because I am so consistent in my ability to forget such things. As a writer, an artist, a romantic, and a dreamer, I spend a lot of my time with my head in the clouds. I'm fortunate to have people like her bring me back to Earth on occasion. Anyway, I want to share a passage from this letter as a lead-in to what I want to say in this chapter. This is what she wrote: "I wish I could have your joy for life and as deep a connection with God. But even though I can't be you, you inspire me every day to be a princess to our King, our God."

I nearly broke down as I read that letter while sitting in a parking lot. It moved me so deeply not just because of how honest and heartfelt it was, but because it made me realize what a man's friendship with a woman can be when God is a part of it, and how I long for all my friendships with the opposite sex to be so rich. Of course, not all my female friends are followers of Christ, and not all of them will be. But as Christ-following men, we can set the example for every female friend or relation we currently have or ever will have. And I think one of the best ways we can do this is to simply be in their lives.

If you were to ask me, I would say that most of my good friends have been women. I am not friends with a good many of them today. I have only recently begun to understand and accept the reality that most of our friendships fade away with time. But any time the bond of friendship was there with those women, it was a special bond. Looking at the current friendships I have with the women in my life in the light of where I am in my journey, with God having set me free from the seemingly indestructible sin of lust, I have found a new purpose in those friendships. I find that it is my heart's desire to tell each of them how beautiful and special they are to me, to encourage them to be proud of who they are as women, and that by God's grace they will see me as a righteous example of the King I serve. I think that's the way God intended friendships between men and women to be. Both should be leading and inspiring one another to be better for the glory of our Savior *as men* and *as women*.

This issue of having relationships with women was not something I expected to focus on when God set me free from lust. It was not something I originally intended to set in this book. Like so many valuable truths, it was so obvious that I missed it. As I began living a life of freedom, God made it clear that being in relationship with women is essential to defeating lust. At first I didn't know why. But as I looked over my female friendships, it became clear. It is essential to our victory over lust because to be in relationship with women is to be consistently faced with the truth that women are human beings.

We live in a world that strips women of humanity every day, and there are few things that make lust appear more attractive than the elimination of humanity. Not a day goes by that a man in our society is not faced with certain messages about women. They say things about her physical beauty, mainly that it is all that matters, that she's really just a body and not much else. Pornography has quite a few messages as well. One of its darker, more insidious messages is that women *want* men to do anything they want to them, no matter how psychopathic or degrading it might be. Whether these messages are oh-so-subtle or in-your-face direct, it's no secret that it is not easy to escape their influence. When a man constantly hears such things, it has the power to affect his behavior toward the opposite sex. And this is where the beauty of relationship really shines. When a man actually befriends a woman and gets to know her, he is faced with the truth. She is not a goddess. She is not a body. She is a person.

I have seen this dynamic played out in my work life over the years. Many times I've seen a female coworker that I want to befriend. I imagine us having coffee. I picture her laughing at my occasional bouts of bizarre verbiage. I create imaginary conversations. This is not a romantic attraction, but simply a desire for building a friendship. It is a blessed reality check when I've managed to succeed. The trap I fall into by viewing her from a distance is that I make her out to be something she isn't. I see her as being purely good, beautiful, charming and lovely. I see no flaws. She is, in every way, altogether wonderful. But when I get the chance to know her, I discover things that distance obscures and friendship illuminates. She isn't perfect. Her life isn't perfect. She has flaws. She fights battles. She carries wounds. She struggles with her identity. She is a human being.

One of the greatest aspects of authentic friendships with the opposite sex is that it teaches us to love them for who they are and not for what our culture says they should be. In lust we browse images and videos of women, ranking them on a scale of attractiveness and desirability. We click a YouTube video because the thumbnail picture shows a sensual cleavage-bearing woman making eye contact with us. We click images or videos based solely on how attractive the woman is – and by how much skin she shows. Before long we are back in that mindset of goddess worship, forgetting the things relationships remind us of. Relationship has a way of acting like an anchor. It always brings us back to the way things really are.

As men, we must love our women *where* they are and for *who* they are – free of judgment, free of comparisons to other women, and free of selfish standard-setting. This kind of love is not always easy. Though we love our friends, they can bother us. Not all of my friends display attributes or beliefs that I agree with or want any part of. Sometimes I am with a group of friends and I have to leave early because the conversation becomes too vulgar. I can't handle it. I don't want to be around it. But they are my friends nonetheless. I don't want to be like them. But I love them. Oh how difficult this dilemma can be.

Once again, we can look to Christ to find out what to do about this. If we look at the sort of people he chose as his disciples and the people he dined with and conversed with, we can see an important theme running through these relationships: he was in relationship with deeply flawed people. He ate dinner and drank wine with sinners. He chatted with a sexually promiscuous woman by a well . . . all by himself. He talked with Gentiles, a people famously abhorrent to Jews. He showed compassion to a woman who had committed adultery, a crime which in those days was punishable by death (it is especially important to see that Jesus showed this compassion *in front of other people*). He begged God to forgive his tormentors as they drove spikes through his wrists. What does this behavior say about our Savior's character? It says that he did not look at people and only acknowledge their failures. He did not measure their worth by what was visible on the outside. He was not concerned with a culture's perception of a specific group. He did not put people into political, personal or cultural boxes and then act on those judgments. He saw these human beings in the light of who they could be if they would only follow him. He loved them in the ways they needed to be loved. This is what we must work towards with our female friends. By loving them in spite of their sins and their faults, we are being Christ to them. This is one of the most powerful ways in which mere boys can grow into men of honor, nobility and strength. How could we want anything less than this?

Of course, we can't be in relationship with every woman we see in our daily lives. It would not surprise me if half the women a man sees every day are in pictures or videos. As unfortunate as it is, something vital is lost when we see an image of a celebrity or a model on the Internet or in newspaper ads or on a magazine cover. We see her face. We see her body. We do not see her for who she is. Her femininity is made less real. Her true self is veiled. We do not see what we as men should seek above all else: her heart. In an image, her humanity is shrouded. But it is not gone. There is a way to reclaim it. When we encounter an image of a woman, we can train ourselves to be reminded of the truth. We must say things like this to ourselves in those moments: "I am looking at a real woman. She bears the image of God. She is real. She is a person. She has fears. She has insecurities. She has been deeply wounded. She is beautiful. She is loved by God." Though we may never be in relationship with these women, we can honor them by telling ourselves that they are more than a cover on a magazine or a series of pixels on our screens.

As for the women you *do* know, what you need to do is quite clear: Make the women in your life feel like princesses to our King by your attitudes, actions and words. So many of us lament that we need to be better at appreciating the people in our lives. I am here to tell you that the time for lamenting is over. Stop wishing and start appreciating. Let the women in your life know how much of a blessing they are to you. Hold the door open for them. Buy them coffee. Protect them. Pray for them in person or in private. Send encouraging notes. Speak loving words. Give them hugs. Care for their hearts. Let them know that the things that matter to them matter to you. Tell them they are beautiful. Read books on godly femininity. Find out what it's like to be a woman in this fallen world. Discover the things that speak to a woman's heart. Learn about the internal trials and struggles women face. Be servants. Learn how to help the women in your life cultivate the gentle and quiet spirit that God finds so valuable. In short, be the greatest student of womanhood the world has ever known.

If you have the desire to be married, this is the best school you can possibly go to in preparation for how you should one day treat your wife. Having ladies for friends is much more than the definitive training for marriage, however. It is training for life. God created men and women to do life together in unity. As much as modern femininity has leaned toward independence and self-reliance apart from men (sometimes aggressively so), this is not how God created it to be. No matter how much the world will try to deny it, women need men and men need women. We no longer seem to understand, accept and appreciate just how much we absolutely *need* each other. Our culture preaches against this. God does not.

> In the Lord, however, woman is not independent of man, nor is man independent of woman. For as woman came from man, so also man is born of woman. But everything comes from God (I Corinthians 11:11-12).

God says that masculinity and femininity belong together. They have *always* belonged together. He was the Author of gender and all its differences. Friendship with a man gives me things friendship with a woman does not. This is not a bad thing. It is wonderful. Each gender has countless blessings for the other according to their God-given sexuality. As God restores your masculinity from the wasteland of lust, you can be reborn as a Christ-following man that the women of the world so desperately need. Women sometimes use the phrase "He thinks he's God's gift to women!" to describe self-centered womanizers who should never be considered true men. Praise God that we can be more. By being Christ to the women in your life, they will say this instead: "He *is* God's gift to women."

I pray that God will guide you away from the wasteland forever and take you into the lush and wonderful pastures of female relationship for a lifetime.

May God bless your lady friends through you.

May those women in your life be a blessing to you.

May they feel like princesses to our King when they are around you.

I find it ironic that I have been working on this chapter around Thanksgiving. It reminds me of just how thankful I am for these relationships I have had and do have with women. I am *deeply* thankful. But I see something deeper at work when I find myself expressing thanks to God for those wonderful women he has placed in my life. These relationships do not cause me to simply be thankful. The reality and the blessing of these relationships causes me to turn to God in worship. And when I worship, I am drawn into amazing closeness with the one whose relationship I must never lose: my Savior.

One of the most powerful ways to cultivate relationship with Christ is worship. I believe that worship is the greatest weapon we have against Satan and all his demonic forces. When I enter that place where there is only praise, delight, and adoration of my Savior, Satan's power is rendered obsolete. Intimacy blossoms, the evils of the world fade away, and I come alive. Music is a huge tool for worship in my own life, but it is not the only tool I have or need. All it takes is telling God from your heart, "I love you." He has given us a world filled with reasons to fall to our knees and cry, "Holy is your name in all the earth!"

At the end of my war, God took me back to one of those reasons. What he took me back to turned out to be the very thing that helped begin the war when I was young. But this time was different. God removed the veil of sin I had placed over it and revealed it for what he always intended it to be – a powerful reminder of why he deserves to be worshiped in the first place.

The Female Form

When I was in the tenth grade, I took a Food Preparation class for my second semester (quite ironic, considering that I hate cooking like I hate watching golf). One day I arrived to class early and I decided to kill some time by doing what I always do when I arrive someplace early: read a book. Reading remains my ultimate weapon against boredom to this day. On this particular day my book of choice was a book about crop circles. Crop circles have fascinated me ever since I first saw *Signs* back in 2002. As I read, a few other high school boys came in. They saw me reading, and one of them asked if it was a book about crop circles. "Yeah," I replied. The boy who asked then turned to a member of his posse and said with a you-know-what-I'm-sayin' tone, "If only they made a crop circle of a naked girl!" Insert laughs and high-fives of approval all around. Insert my disapproving nonchalance.

Looking back on this incident years later makes me want to imagine how else I might have replied to those guys. If I was the man I am now and this same episode occurred, I would have asked that boy one question: "Why? Why would you choose a naked girl to be artistically represented in a field of corn?" To which the reply would probably be along the lines of "Uh . . . because naked girls are hot!" My reason for wanting to ask a question like that is simple: I want to see what lies at the heart of the shallow answer. I want to discover what is *really* going on when a man says things like this.

We must do the same thing with the issue of lust in our lives. We must go deeper. To arrive triumphant at the place in our souls where God has the ability to expose the lies, engrave truth on the tablets of our hearts, and ultimately set us free from lust, we *have* to go far deeper than "Stop masturbating," "Stop looking at porn," "Stop ogling." Freedom from lust cannot happen by treating the symptoms and ignoring the disease. People who suffer from chronic sins and addictions don't receive healing by deciding one day to call it quits. You cannot simply decide to be free from an addiction. Freedom only happens on the outside when it has first happened from within. When it comes to lust, it happens when we see beauty for what it truly is.

I think human beings possess two types of beauty: physical beauty and heart beauty. We all have both in different measures. Throughout my life, I've seen the church address the beauty of the heart many times, with I Peter 3:3-4 being used to make the point. The verses speak very clearly about inner beauty being of greatest worth in the eyes of God, and how it should be with his followers. I agree with this passage. I believe the beauty of the heart is what a man should always seek, protect, and cultivate when he finds himself drawn to a woman. As I look back, however, I see one thing quite clear: the other of the two beauties was given little to no emphasis at all. As I grow older, not much has changed.

This entire chapter can be summed up in this one truth: Physical beauty matters. *It matters.* Yes, we can be led astray by it. Yes, men and women can place it above heart beauty all too often. Yes, we can too easily judge a person's worth based solely upon it. Physical beauty can matter too much to us for all the wrong reasons. So why did God create it? If it was not important, God would not have created human beings – especially women – to be so pleasing to the eye. It seems to me that physical beauty mattered to God in the beginning and still matters to him now. It would seem that God clearly had things on his mind when he bestowed physical beauty on human beings at the dawn of creation.

I think a great place for we men to begin our healing would be to ask ourselves the all-important question: Why? As you read the questions below, don't just give them a quick response and move on. Really *think* about your answers.

Why does the physical beauty of a woman's body matter?

Why does a woman's beauty seem to follow us almost everywhere we go?

Why does the female body have so much power over the heart of man?

Why have we turned the female body into an idol to which we surrender everything?

And the most important question of all:

Why is the female body so beautiful?

Why?

Could it be that God is trying to use this beauty to tell his men something?

Could it be that Satan is trying to steal and pervert what God is trying to tell us?

Could it be that the very thing that causes men to lust is also the very thing that has the power to save them?

> They came to Bethsaida, and some people brought a blind man and begged Jesus to touch him. He took the blind man by the hand and led him outside the village. When he had spit on the man's eyes and put his hands on him, Jesus asked, "Do you see anything?" He looked up and said, "I see people; they look like trees walking around." Once more Jesus put his hands on the man's eyes. Then his eyes were opened, his sight was restored, and he saw everything clearly (Mark 8:22-25).

This passage is very insightful when we apply it to this issue of lust in the world. You will notice when Jesus first touches the man's eyes, he can see, but not very well. When he looks at people, they look like "trees walking around." We are very much like this man when we are trapped in a cycle of lust. Our sight is not completely gone, but our vision is impaired by sinful deceit. We see a woman's body not for what it is in reality, but only for what it appears to be. It appears to be a thing as opposed to a being. And the world has accepted this veiled view as the standard. When a man looks at a woman's body with lust in his heart, she is nothing more than a tree walking around. The truth is hidden. But then we look at the second portion of the miracle.

When the man says his vision is not fully restored, Jesus does not walk away discouraged. He does not accept this as the sad reality. *Jesus is not content with leaving the man in that broken state.* He does not want him to go through life with truth blocked from his sight, never seeing anything for what it really is. He touches him again. Immediately the man's eyes are fully opened. The blindfold has come off. He now sees what is real and true.

This episode is a perfect picture of how our healing from lust can happen. It does not happen with staying half-blind. It does not come from remaining behind the veil. It happens when our eyes are fully opened by the only One who can fully open them.

In the art of cinema, there is a narrative technique called a bookend. It is when two similar shots or scenes take place at the beginning and end of a film. Sometimes it's the exact same shot (a famous example is the shots of the candles in *Schindler's List,* or the beginnings and endings of *Road To Perdition, Gone Girl,* and *A River Runs Through It,* just to name a few). Filmmakers sometimes use bookends as a way of bringing the story full-circle and providing a unifying sense of closure. That is exactly what God did with me. He used similar images to bookend the first part of my story. Where the first ones led to a massive war for my soul, the second ones brought about my glorious rescue. Those images were of the female body.

God did not free me from lust by sending me to a cave. He did not tell me to become the prior of a monastery. He did not destroy my computer. He did not come to me in a dream and declare, "You shall never look upon women again." No. God set me free by bringing me back to the body of Eve herself. The way he did this was very unique.

Just days after going through the door to freedom, I found myself drawn to paintings. I was especially drawn to the paintings of the artists William Bouguereau and John William Waterhouse. The former painted many scenes from classical mythology while anchoring his work in the realist tradition. During his lifetime, Bouguereau was wealthy, beloved by his associates and students and famous in his native France and the United States. The latter painted in a style known as Pre-Raphaelite, and depicted many scenes from mythology and Arthurian literature. Due to his less-documented personal life and his decisions to paint in styles that were not in fashion during his career, Waterhouse did not become well-known until after his death in 1917. These two prolific artists from two different countries produced a vast portion of their work in the latter half of the 1800s. Though different in many ways, they both had a common subject in their work. Both artists specialized in painting female beauty.

This part of my journey into freedom amazes me whenever I think about it. From birth to the present, I have always been able to draw. But I have never been able to paint. Before my freedom I never studied the craft with profound enthusiasm. I could admire and appreciate the craft of a good painting and identify some works and names. But I could never see the soul of the art itself, the nameless aspects of the heart of the artist that he or she had delicately applied with a paintbrush to the canvas. Now all of a sudden I was looking at this incredible artwork and finding myself completely enamored, like a person is when they discover a hidden treasure that was right there in front of them the whole time. In the thick of the war, seeking out such images would have been disastrous. It would not have mattered if they were paintings or photos. Images like these had the power to awaken lustful desire. It had happened before. But not this time.

In that moment something monumental shifted inside me.

Something unheard of happened as I rediscovered the beauty of Eve through art.

It was as if I was beholding the beauty of a woman's body for the first time.

What I felt was not lust. Lust was nowhere to be found.

All I felt instead was the awe I feel when I encounter God.

In that moment God granted me a taste of the freedom that changed my life.

I'm going to ask you to do something for a quick minute. Grab a pen and paper and write down all the descriptive words that come to your mind when you think of the words "female body." I'll give you some of mine. I would not be surprised if a lot of us are thinking the same things:

- Captivating
- Beautiful
- Haunting
- Sensual
- Breathtaking
- Gorgeous
- Graceful
- Arresting
- Poetic
- Gentle
- Tender
- Precious
- Peaceful
- Alluring
- Powerful
- Serene
- Awe-inspiring

I could go on all day. But then I would need to write another book.

Looking back over my story (and your own stories), you would think I had learned all I needed to know about the female body. I had seen every angle and corner and curve of Eve's form by the war's end. But when he set me free, God revealed that in that twelve-year span of time there was much about the female body I never saw at all. In my lust I saw the female form as something else altogether. Lust is such an enticing sin because it causes us to see a woman with only *our* eyes. I would go so far as to argue that the look we give the female form is the very soil in which lust has the potential to grow for us visually-oriented men. All it takes is one look at her form, and from that look the heart begins to perform its work for good or for evil. The look is everything. But the fact remains that men cannot escape women for the sake of purity, leaving the problem of lust staring us down almost everywhere we go. This is where the news gets good. It is also from that single glance at her body – whether in person or in an image, whether clothed or unclothed – where we can kill lust at the root. And I am not suggesting we turn a blind eye.

When God decides it's time for me to go home, I really want to ask him a question when I get there. I have a lot to ask him, actually, but this particular question has to be in the top three. I get this vision of both of us walking through the fields of Paradise together, running our hands through the wheat like Maximus, watching birds fly across the heavenly skies, and I look over and ask him, "God, what was on your mind when you designed the female body?" I can't wait to get his actual face-to-face reply. But I can imagine what it might be. I can hear God taking me back to the words of Romans 1:20 in a deep but tender voice: "Scott, I put myself into everything I made at creation. My character – my heart – has been made known through the work of my hands so that no one can say that they do not know who I am. One of those works of creation, the one that I saved for last, is the female body."

I must admit that sometimes I selfishly wish I could pass away so I can have this particular conversation with God. But there is still much work to be done for the kingdom, so I'll stick around.

The glorious healing for our sin-damaged hearts must begin first and foremost with this biblical truth: A woman is made in the image of God. We have heard this many times. Yet how many of us have actually stopped and truly given thought to what that means? Let us move past our numbness and really *look* at this reality. A woman is made in the image of the Almighty God. God did not create nature in his image. He did not bestow the expanse of the universe with the gift of his likeness. The natural world has enormous beauty. But all the beauty on Earth does not compare to the beauty of Eve. All the rolling hills and windswept fields of the Palouse countryside cannot equal the contours of the female breast. The songs of all the birds in nature do not move us like the sound of a woman's voice. Staring at all the stars and celestial bodies in the dark of night does not hold a candle to staring directly into the eyes of a woman you are attracted to or married to. The wonder we feel when standing before the Grand Canyon does not affect our souls as deeply as beholding the unclothed female body. Why? Why does nothing else in all the world compare to her? Because nothing else in all creation is made directly in the image of the One who created it. The fact that she is one of only two beings in the entire universe to be made directly in God's holy image speaks volumes about what is in the heart of our king.

The female body is all the adjectives listed above and so much more because that is how the Artist crafted it at creation. Like any artist does when creating a work of art, God put himself into what he made. This is powerfully apparent when we look at the beauty of a woman's body. Her skin, her feet, her legs, her thighs, her vagina, her clitoris, her pubic hair, her waist, her navel, her breasts, her face, her eyes, her locks of hair, the delicate way these wonders weave together as a seamless whole to produce one sensual and curvaceous form – all these exceedingly beautiful things our world has idolized, defiled, and claimed for itself were God's ideas. God was the author of everything about a woman's body that causes a man's eyes to stop and take notice. The way her body moves, the way her face looks when she closes her eyes and smiles, the way God designed sunlight to fall on her, the way God causes the wind to blow over her, the way God created light and shadow to wrap around her – it is plain and clear that God specifically designed the female body to do nothing if not make us *pay attention*. It is one of the great themes that God inscribed into feminine beauty at the dawn of creation. *Stop. Pay attention. Look closer.*

What we men need to reclaim and hold onto forever is the truth that the beauty of a woman's body is wonderfully and profoundly *good*. Every time you behold a woman's body, you are beholding something that is utterly good. It is astonishing beyond words how good the beauty of Eve's body is. In spite of all the brokenness that comes from our selfish choices, in spite of all the evil we fallen humans commit against God and one another, her beauty is still good – just like the one who created her. *Idolize it. Deify it. Take it. Possess it. Mock it. Destroy it.* This is the world's experience of feminine beauty. This is what runs through the world's mind when it portrays a woman's body. God's experience is much different. It is summed up in a single word we see at the end of all the verses in Genesis that speak of what he created. *Good.* If we sons of God would only stand back and allow ourselves to just *feel* a sense of awe at the beauty of her physical form, to just behold her and allow your breath to be taken away, I don't think we would be able to comprehend the kind of healing the Artist could bring to our hearts. This is not lust, men. This is freedom.

I never heard anything like this from the church when the issue of lust was discussed. The idea of men thanking God for and inspiring one another to thank God for feminine beauty was all but nonexistent. I heard many times things along the lines of "Hands and eyes off." I didn't hear the church telling its women anything more than the mixed message, "You are so beautiful that you must hide it." I believe in modesty and chastity and abstinence, honorable traits that we must cherish and uphold like the treasures they are. But when have women ever heard anyone in the church say that their bodies are any of the attributes on the above list? When has the church encouraged its women to thank God for the beauty of their physical bodies? This is the current situation: Christian men are encouraged to avoid the physical beauty of Eve, and Christian women are encouraged to keep it well-hidden. It seems that for the most part, the church is confused about, judgmental about, critical of, afraid of, embarrassed by and ashamed of the female body. The most subtle and dangerous aspect of what this kind of climate fosters in the hearts of men is the lie that when a man beholds a woman's body, what he is looking at is not good. The very thing he beholds is evil.

I am going to rabbit-trail for a minute by providing an example (just an example, nothing more) that illustrates what I am trying to illuminate – pole dancing. Pole dancing is a performance art that takes an astonishing level of training, endurance and athletic skill. The female performers are not only performers but athletes, having the type of physicality we usually think of when discussing the Olympics. Watching a pole dancer, you can see in the complexity of their movements just how many endless hours of practice and training goes into a deceptively simple routine that lasts maybe a few minutes. The women don't wear much because the unrestricted smoothness of their bodies is required to execute the complex maneuvers. They do not use their bodies for seduction, but for illumination. Pole dancing is one of those art forms that only seems to reach its greatest potential when it is performed by women, an art that not only draws attention to the grace of their athleticism, but the beauty of their bodies in motion. In the purest definition, pole dancers are athletic artists using a particular type of art as a means to express the soul. It is a truly stunning vision of the feminine.

When you read the words "pole dancing," I'm guessing it conjured up images of strip clubs, prostitutes, rave music, and guys throwing sweaty wads of dog-eared money. Throughout history, pole dance has been used by ungodly women inside ungodly places in the service of ungodly sins, and ungodly men have watched it for ungodly reasons. Therefore, in the light of these realities, it is only logical to think that pole dancing itself is evil. But it's not. Remove it from that sinful world and what you are left with is something incredible. When lust takes over, not a single element of what I just stated above is possible to see. All that breathtaking beauty becomes invisible. That is what lust does. It does not allow us to see the beauty in anything.

Satan is a master at taking the beautiful and blinding us to it through corrupted desire. Never is this more apparent than with the body of Eve. His tactic with destroying her beauty is aimed at two groups: the world and the church. He convinces the world that her beauty is something to consume and defile without shame or guilt.

He convinces the church that her beauty should be buried because it is lethal. His tactic has worked. The world has desecrated the female body to the point where we hardly recognize it for what it is. The church has put "Do Not Cross" signs all around the female body and convinced its men that it is dangerous and only capable of awakening wickedness in our hearts. In this present age, Christian men have been led to believe that acknowledging anything other than a woman's face is wrong, as if everything else about her body is the work of the devil.

We can break free from these chains by remembering the truth of the Word: whatever God made was good in the beginning, and it will remain good forever. This includes the body of Eve. When God was creating the female breast, the labia, the waist, the hair, the eyes and everything else about her that captures a man's soul, he was not making any mistakes. He was not embarrassed when he was pouring his heart and soul into the female form, sculpting every delicate curve and engrossing texture, giving her all those smooth and sensuous lines that will never cease to take the world's breath away. In all the years you have lived on Earth, whenever you beheld a woman's body, you never once beheld something that caused God to turn away in shame. You never beheld something that was designed to seduce you to the ways of the sinful nature. No way. You beheld his pride and adoration. You beheld the beloved work of the Potter's hands. You beheld Beauty incarnate. The female body is not evil. Why? Because all those adjectives I listed above are true of the God we serve, and they are all true about the female body, an artwork God crafted in his eternally captivating likeness.

Nakedness

It's interesting to me as I try to recall the times in my life when I discussed lust with another man or a group of men. Two things stand out to me about these conversations. First, they were always private. Of course. How else does one talk about so sensitive a topic? Second, I find myself remembering more what was *not* talked about than what was. One of those undiscussed topics was nakedness. It makes sense. At that point in my life, there was no point in talking about it. Nudity was an open-and-shut case. The lines were clearly drawn, and those lines were never to be crossed for any reason. *To behold a naked body is sin* is a belief the church has long held close, and for the longest time, I felt the same way. It wasn't discussed because it was clearly wrong.

I mentioned earlier about what it was like to behold the beauty of Eve in art after God set me free. It was unknown to me at the time, but in that process God was teaching me a few things about nudity. One of those things was the fact that nudity need not be a topic we skirt around and refuse to bring up. I think it's time we discussed it for two reasons: we have unlimited access to nudity in our world today, and Christians believe things about it that aren't true. Thinking about it now, I find the subject of nudity to be a bit of a paradox. It is very important, and yet not important at all. In order to rethink nudity and approach it with fresh eyes, we must turn to the best resource we have: the book of Genesis.

Adam and Eve were both naked, and they felt no shame. In an atmosphere of innocence they beheld each other's bodies as God always intended. Then the serpent came to tempt them both, and their choices brought about the Fall. The verse that immediately follows the eating of the fruit is insightful. The first thing that happened was not a tangible cosmic shifting of the universe. The earth did not erupt in earthquakes, twisters and volcanic eruptions. The celestial bodies did not suddenly implode on themselves. No. Adam and Eve saw their naked bodies and something inside their hearts shifted. Suddenly, they looked at each other and shame was all they knew. They no longer looked at one another and said, "I am in awe." They now said, "I have to hide." They were so ashamed that the first thing they did after the Fall was cover themselves. They hid from each other the only things in the entire universe that directly bore the image of the God of the universe.

In looking at this story, we can see right away why shame became inseparable with nudity after the Fall. I think it can also help us to see clothing in a new light. Genesis 3:21 tells us that God made clothing for them after the curse of sin was pronounced. In all honesty, I think he was deeply wounded by the fact that he was now covering something that he did not intend to keep covered. It was a generous act of humility on God's part to give us clothing after shame was introduced by the Fall. Since then humankind has simply worn clothing without much thought to it. We wear clothes. It is the way it is. But looking at the Genesis account a little closer reveals something we tend to overlook: it was not part of God's original design.

Now, I'm not advocating we never clothes. I'm not saying a person's conversion to Christianity should also be a conversion to nudism. While clothing is not some evil that must be purged from the earth, it does two things that have subtle but very negative outcomes. First and foremost, clothing blocks from our sight the beauty of our physical bodies that bear God's holy image. In many ways, it teaches us to fear and be uncomfortable with what lies beneath the fabric. For some men, lust has greater potential to be awoken by clothing because it can cause the mind to fantasize beyond a healthy curiosity about what lies beneath it. A woman in a bikini can be more sexually stimulating than a nude woman for this very reason. Second, clothing divides. There are few things on Earth that have the power to tempt us to judge one another like clothing.

When we see what a person is wearing, it can cause us to make up in our own minds what kind of person we are seeing, despite the fact that we don't know them. Clothing labels us. It puts us in boxes. It stereotypes us. It places us into subcultures and social classes. Yes, it is true that what a person wears says things about them. But we are insufferably naive to think that we truly know who they are based on this rationale.

Look at Genesis before the Fall. Do we see anything like this going on between Adam and Eve before God brought them together in marriage? Do we see them labeling each other? Do we see them looking at one another in revulsion and fear because they are not clothed? *Absolutely not.* In a clothing-free world, Adam and Eve knew the truth, and the truth was that their bodies were created by God to bear his image as male and female in different yet equally powerful ways. Your body, my body, her body . . . they are in equal standing with one another because they were created for the same purpose. Nudity can teach this to us. When we are unclothed, we are as we were at the dawn of creation. Race, religion, personality, social standing, fame, occupation, political views – nudity takes all of this away and forces us to see one another as male and female in the purest way possible.

For too long we have continued to categorize nudity as the epitome of shame when, in reality, it is the epitome of purity. There are few things – maybe *nothing* – more pure and innocent than an unclothed body. And there lies the paradox. It is a huge deal *because* of its purity. It is not a huge deal because it is simply how God created us. It need not be a monumental issue. It need not be an issue at all. Indigenous cultures the world over have known these things inherently for thousands of years. Why are God's people so far behind? Look at God's question that he asks Adam in Genesis: "Who told you you were naked?" Or, to look at it another way: "Why is your nakedness now such a big deal?" Even though we have gotten used to feeling this way about nudity, do we believe God wants us to feel things like shame and revulsion when beholding something he created to be beautiful beyond description?

As men, when we behold a woman's body in any state of dress, it does not have to be a surface-level action we give little thought to. When we look with the eyes of God, beholding the female form can be a deeply profound experience. While it is incredibly sad and unfortunate that the female body has become almost wholly sexualized in our world today, eroticism does not have to be present in an experience of feminine beauty at all. Though the world doesn't seem to have caught on to the realization, the female form is not just "sexual." It is so much more than that. It is pure. It is innocent. It is beautiful. It is good. Encounters with feminine beauty are supposed to reveal and teach these things to us. That is what *all* beauty does. It teaches. It tells us in a soft voice to shut out the lies of the world and to simply sit at its feet and listen to what it has to say about life, about reality, about God, and about ourselves. Encounters with beauty can teach us more about these things than any sermon, if we would only see and listen with the wellspring of life within us. Is there any wonder why Proverbs personifies the virtue of wisdom as a beautiful woman "more precious than rubies?" This is what beholding the female form can be. This is what it *should* be. Instead of being something wrought of lustful desire, it can be born of a hunger to know God. Satan used lust and shame to tell me this kind of holy aesthetic experience I am describing was completely impossible. He convinced me – and countless other men – that the sight of a naked body was an immediate path to perversion and nothing else. I believe God is telling his men otherwise.

Nakedness is no different from anything else in the world in that it can be used for good or used for evil. We've understood the evil since we were young. We now need to understand the good. I am so grateful that amid this age of easily-accessible pornography and sexualized desecration of the female body, there are those rare people who use their artistic gifts to help us see beyond the pollution of our culture. I think the artists have had it right all along. When they painted, sculpted or photographed women as their subjects, I think they knew something the church has sorely missed. In seeing a sculpture or a painting or an artistic photograph of the naked female body, you are seeing it for what it is – an awe-inspiring masterpiece that speaks to the beauty of our sovereign Lord. The artist, even if he or she is not a follower of Christ, celebrates and even honors the beauty of Eve by using art – beauty made from beauty – to draw attention to the God-created artistry of her body, revealing her not as a soulless piece of property for a man to possess, but a captivating human being whose physical beauty inspires genuine awe and deep admiration. In short, art is honest.

This does not sound like pornography to me. Pornography accomplishes the reverse of what art does. In terms of telling men what female beauty really is, pornography could not be more deceitful. When you look at porn, you are not looking at an accurate and truthful portrayal of feminine beauty. When you look at porn, you are not looking at something that exists to help you see beauty, let alone see the human soul beneath the beauty. When we see a woman's body with God's eyes, we will never fail to understand that we are beholding not just a body, but a body with a soul – a person with a past, a life, hurts, loves, hopes, dreams, and, of course, a profound beauty. The belief that every image of female nudity should be classified as pornography is simply not true. As Christian men, we *have* to stop thinking that just because we see a naked or thinly-dressed female we are instantly committing the sin of lust.

This is especially important to understand when we take our biological urges into account. Let me offer two scenarios. Scenario 1: You are in an art museum. You peruse all the magnificent paintings, sculptures and photographs. You see many that depict the female nude, and sometimes you feel a sexual response to the artwork. Scenario 2: You're at the beach in the thick of summer. Women are everywhere, and most of them are wearing bikinis. You, being a man, notice these ladies' bodies. You don't stare and ogle like an alleyway pervert, but nonetheless you feel aroused. Now, most of us would look at these scenarios and think "lust." Our old companions Shame and Guilt come back to us with a vengeance. "I feel aroused, therefore I must be lusting." Since lust and sexual arousal are so closely linked in the minds of many men, they feel they have no choice but to adopt this mindset as stone-tablet truth. It is because of this belief that many men are afraid of their sexual response to a woman's beauty. It brings me great joy to tell you, my brothers, that our arousal is not the problem. The problem is how we've been interpreting it.

I want us to do something bold right now. Let us remove our guilt, our fear and our shame and just come out and admit it: We men are sexually aroused by a woman's body. There! Don't you feel better about telling the elephant in the room to take a hike? Now that we've admitted what has been obvious all along, we must look at this truth about our sexual arousal at feminine beauty and stop pretending like it doesn't exist. Many men feel they have to in order to remain pure. This is foolish. To even attempt to deny the existence of sexual arousal at the sight of feminine beauty is to willingly charge into a battle you will always lose. I once heard a piece of advice about sexual purity that went something like this: "Avoid any image of a woman that causes an erection." What do you think such advice tells you about your sexuality as a man? Does this teach you to embrace your sexuality or to hate it?

As difficult as it is for many of us to believe, our sexual response at the sight of feminine beauty is a very good thing. It was another tile God added to the mosaic of our manhood. Contrary to what your enemy wants you and I to believe and what many women sadly believe, there is nothing repulsive about a man's sexual arousal. It is nothing to be afraid of. It is not something we should want to wish away. Rather, it is a vital part of our masculinity that we must learn to understand, and ultimately, to embrace. I believe that much of the sexual shame men feel is a result of thinking biological sexual arousal and lust are one and the same. But when we can clearly see that one is from God and the other is from hell, we take back enormous sexual ground the enemy has stolen from us. One of the greatest ways a man can bring healing to his sexuality is to simply thank God for it. "Thank you, Father, for giving me a sex drive. Thank you for creating me to notice a woman's body. Thank you, God, for creating me to be sexually aroused by the female body." These are beautiful things to pray.

I began to do something like this a couple years ago. I have a daily prayer that I like to pray at the start of my day. I've changed it and added to it off and on, but one thing I always incorporate is thanksgiving for my sexuality, my sex drive, and the sexual desires of my mind and heart. Brothers, I have known unimagined freedom in making this a regular part of my life. It has brought me so much peace and assurance when I remind myself through prayer that my sexuality and all that comes with it is good. The enemy loses his chances of victory over our hearts and minds when we listen to the voice of truth.

There is also another side of this to examine. We can look at a woman's body and not have anything sexual happen at all. Contrary to popular myth, not all men instantly think sexual thoughts when seeing a beautiful woman. Arousal doesn't always happen. Like I said before, when it comes to viewing the female body, sex isn't everything. So what about those times where we *do* feel those urges? While it is true that those urges may sometimes be present when we see women who catch our eye, we must be careful not to confuse arousal with desire. Arousal is what happens to our bodies. Desire is what happens to our hearts. They are different.

If we see a woman in daily life or in imagery and we feel sexual urges, that does not mean that our heart's desire is to have her at all costs. It does not mean that husbands want to forsake their wives for a night of adulterous pleasures. It does not mean that we now want to go off and masturbate to her. It doesn't even mean that we are looking for the sole purpose of experiencing sexual arousal. It is vital to our healing and our freedom that we understand these differences. *The way a man's genitalia react to the sight of female beauty has absolutely nothing to do with the desires of his heart.* When we behold the beauty of a woman's body, we should never focus on how our bodies are responding. We should instead be focusing on how our *hearts* are responding. In seeing feminine beauty in art or in life, our hearts are stirred. *Why* our hearts are stirred at the sight of her body and what happens as a result is the field where the devil and God wage war.

God created the female form. He crafted it with the precision and passion of the most dedicated Artist in the universe. It was all his idea. God created Eve to be utterly breathtaking, and what he created he called "good." We understand this now. What we now need to understand is that these truths are where our eyes, our minds, and our hearts have needed to be the whole time. When seeing a woman in everyday life, it is easy to acknowledge how gorgeous she is because she is physically right there before us. By all means, we should recognize and appreciate her beauty. But the beauty of a woman's body should not be the only thing we are drawn to in that moment. *An experience of feminine beauty should always cause us to recognize and acknowledge the beauty of the Artist.* Where the potential for lust is present every time we look at a woman's body in any state of dress, so too is the potential for genuine awe, honor and wonder at the beauty of our God when we look upon her.

This is how I was ultimately freed from the cycle of lustful behavior, and how I believe other men can be freed as well. When we behold Eve we cannot forsake God, for without God's beauty we do not have Eve's beauty. Try to think back over your life and remember the most captivating women you have ever seen. The beauty of those women who left you so entranced would not exist at all without God. Husbands, the beauty of your wives is only there because of God. *She* is only there because of God. Writing this down makes me clearly see how unthinkable it would be for me *not* to acknowledge God when seeing female beauty. How unthinkable to not acknowledge *his* beauty!

Since God set me free, every time I see a woman whose beauty catches my eye or touches my heart, I try to say two things: "God, thank you," and "God, you are so (attributes from the list)." The best part is that there are women everywhere. I have a chance to do this multiple times a day, whether quietly out loud or in my soul. I cannot begin to describe what this will do for your spiritual life. Few things will make God seem more utterly real. For the first two months after

I was set free, my spiritual life was even better than when I first fell in love with God back when I was eighteen. I can take those things into my heart and say things like "God, you are so captivating. You are so haunting. You are so graceful. You are so good."

The word *arouse* is often used when describing sexuality. But the word's meaning causes me to see everything I am talking about in a new light. The definition of arouse is "to awaken." It calls forth the truth of a woman's body being so beautiful that it has the power to literally *awaken* men to God. Everything that moves me and all the beautiful things in my life can *arouse* me to the Artist who created it. This entire world is filled to the point of bursting with incredible monuments to his loving goodness. Ever since he set me free I cannot help but say, "Wow, God! Men are truly without excuse!"

For twelve years I thought lust was a better option than this.

This is all wonderful news. But as wonderful as it is, we must remember the state of the world we live in before we go out and start looking at every woman who comes across our path. In the same way that the female body itself was damaged by the Fall, so too was the way in which men *view* the female body. This fallen view currently has the world firmly in its grasp. God can set us free from this lustful view and give us the eyes to see a woman's body as he always intended, regardless of her state of dress, but this does not change the fact that our world is deeply broken.

Because we live in a world caught between heaven and hell, I am not advocating, nor do I believe, that men now have free reign to indulge to their eye's and soul's content. Nor am I saying women should forsake modesty in light of how wonderful their bodies are. If a woman is a follower of Christ, I believe that what she wears is between her and God (I greatly admire women who have the courage to bring their wardrobe to God, given the amount of pressure our world puts on them to be physically beautiful or just to 'fit in'). Modesty is a great teacher. It shows us that physical beauty is not humanity's alpha and omega. The point is this: all men, married or single, must learn to honor and respect the female form no matter how well-clothed it is. This happens when we see her with the eyes of the Artist. For this to happen, we need to be healed.

We must also never forget that Satan is the master when it comes to selling goodness in slavery to wickedness. As deeply precious and profoundly beautiful as it is, the female body can be a conduit for evil like nothing else on the face of the earth. Nothing has the power to corrupt men like the body of Eve. Scripture is filled with a constant awareness of this reality (just look at Proverbs 5 and 7). When we see a woman who catches our eye, Satan makes every attempt to jump in with his lies and accusations and twist that moment towards evil. Where lust has a chance to spread like a virus is when we look at a woman's body and listen to what our enemy whispers, when we only think about what *we* are getting from it for ourselves as opposed to turning towards her more infinitely beautiful Creator. Lust says about a woman, "Her body is what you are really after because that's all she is." Lust takes the beauty of God completely out of the experience of seeing her and tells us that it is only her physical body we should be focusing on, that her body is the actual beauty we long to possess. Why? Because it's all for us, and our pleasure should always be top priority.

A vast majority of the images we see of women encourage us to maintain this sinful way of thinking. This is why we do not have unlimited visual access. This twisted mindset has to be transformed into one that puts God first in all things. The sinful nature has to be destroyed. Thanks be to God that we do not have to rely on our own strength to achieve holiness! Thanks be to Jesus that we can do this through his strength which resides in us!

I want to close this chapter with two passages of Scripture. For Christian men who struggle with lust, they may be familiar. We can probably quote them by heart at this point.

Don't you know that you yourselves are God's temple and that God's Spirit dwells in your midst? If anyone destroys God's temple, God will destroy that person; for God's temple is sacred, and you together are that temple (1 Corinthians 3:16-17).

Flee from sexual immorality. All other sins a person commits are outside the body, but whoever sins sexually, sins against their own body. Do you not know that your bodies are temples of the Holy Spirit, who is in you, whom you have received from God? You are not your own; you were bought at a price. Therefore honor God with your bodies (1 Corinthians 6:18-20).

I am going to point something out that I believe we have either missed or given too little thought to. Both verses speak of temples. Our physical bodies individually are temples, and together we as followers of Christ make up one temple, the church. The spirit of God dwells within us as individuals and as one body when we give our lives and hearts to Christ. Together and individually, the male body and the female body represent God's image and divine character in ways unique to our God-given sexuality. When we picture men's bodies, we think of things associated with strength and might. When we picture a woman's body, just look at our list. I find it fascinating that Paul chose the word "temple" as the metaphor in these verses. A temple has always been seen as and used for a house of worship, a place where we go to be in God's holy presence. We go to a temple to experience God. Scripture tells us we must honor God with our bodies. But have we ever at any moment in our lives thought about going farther than this? Have we not only considered honoring God *with* our bodies, but have we also considered honoring God *because* of our bodies? Have we men ever looked at a woman's body – clothed or unclothed, in life or in art – and done the very things we go to a temple to do?

Think about nature for a moment. I mentioned earlier that nature is everywhere in the Bible when it comes to describing aspects of God's character and how we long to be near him.

But blessed is the one who trusts in the LORD,
whose confidence is in him.
They will be like a tree planted by the water
that sends out its roots by the stream.
It does not fear when heat comes;
its leaves are always green.
It has no worries in a year of drought
and never fails to bear fruit (Jeremiah 17:7-8).

As the deer pants for streams of water,
so my soul pants for you, my God (Psalm 42:1).

The heavens declare the glory of God;
the skies proclaim the work of his hands.
Day after day they pour forth speech;
night after night they reveal knowledge (Psalm 19:1-4).

The voice of the LORD is over the waters;
the God of glory thunders,
the LORD thunders over the mighty waters.
The voice of the LORD is powerful;
the voice of the LORD is majestic.
The voice of the LORD breaks the cedars;
the LORD breaks in pieces the cedars of Lebanon (Psalm 29:3-5).

God designed nature from its inception to be an enormous house of praise. Not just praise, but pure, unbridled passion. References to fruits, spices, animals, mountains and vineyards abound in the highly erotic Songs of Songs. Writers and poets use nature similes in an attempt to describe the indescribable (something awesome and beautiful is "like a river," "like a mountain," "like a forest"). When I stood at the edge of the Grand Canyon on my road trip back in 2010, I was unable to speak. The fact that something so vast – so *present* – could exist on this earth right there before my eyes was more than words could hope to capture. I've always thought the ocean was nature's greatest representation of God: a terrifying and ferocious place, and yet a place of unprecedented tranquility. Animals cover all corners of the earth, each one unique and special in its own way, many of which have still to be discovered. One of my non-believing friends told me about her time in Zion National Park and how just looking at all the wonders contained within caused her to say, "God did this." It is an undeniable truth that for most Christians, being in nature makes us turn back to God. It makes us *worship*.

Picture a cathedral. I remember standing inside Notre Dame when my family and I visited Europe back in 2009. I still cannot believe that fallen mankind could be capable of creating a structure so awe-inspiring. So worshipful. Most cathedrals took decades, sometimes centuries to build. Masters of every architectural craft and art contributed to their finished design. These people knew what kind of structure they were building, and as such they all but guaranteed their work would be of the highest quality. Look at any picture of the inside of one, and you will see so much intricate detail in every pillar, altar, balustrade and buttress that it will make your eyes hurt. Cathedrals have incredibly high ceilings. The purpose of their enormous height is to metaphorically draw our eyes upward toward heaven. As well it should. A cathedral is one of the most stunning monuments of worship that exists on Earth.

But there is another out there even more stunning than both of these examples combined, something no man or empire could ever hope to build, something all the wonder in nature cannot equal. It is a living monument we can see with the eyes of the Artist every day as a reminder of his good and powerful greatness, one of only two things in all creation to directly bear his likeness. It's the physical body of Eve, a form that God created to be so awe-inspiring, captivating, haunting, and sensual, that all it takes is a single look to cause us to fall to our knees and say, "O holy God, how good and beautiful you are!"

What do you think is the most popular subject of poetry? What brings more inspiration to artists of all mediums across the world? What seems to appear in paintings more than any other subject? One time I was searching Google Images and I randomly typed the word "beauty." Take a guess as to what appeared more than any other subject. Why do you think the word "lust" is so closely associated with the female form? Other than Christ himself and perhaps sexual intimacy, what has been more violated, abused and outright destroyed? There is no denying the obvious: a woman's body is an artwork of tremendous power. The most powerful in all the world. But in reality, Eve's beauty is a dim reflection. She is but one of many rivers that flow from the one and only Spring. How often have we tried to drink from the river when the Spring has been calling to us the whole time?

Think of all the incredible praise songs written down through time, songs that were written by people with a passion for our Savior that can only be expressed in song, of what it feels like to sing said songs in unison with the multitudes of God's people. Think back to the most profound experience of God's presence you have ever had. All those songs that talk about the love and might of the great I Am beloved by so many Christians the world over? They are talking about the same I Am who used his artist's hands to knit the female body together in the secret place. The One whose presence you felt in those powerful experiences was the same One who poured his naked heart into the sacred gift of feminine beauty for all the world to see. The God who placed one trillion stars in the Andromeda Galaxy is the same God who placed a unique and vibrant soul into every woman you have ever seen, every one of them different and special and set apart from all others. The God who parted the Red Sea to set a nation free, the God who is seated in splendor on the throne of his eternal kingdom, the God who sent his one and only son to die for the sins of the world – he is the same God who makes his captivating beauty known to us every day through the precious beauty of Eve.

This is why we as men must bring the Artist all the glory for giving us this most fearfully and wonderfully-made masterwork. We *must*. For too long we have only thought about and acted on what a woman's body gives us rather than what it can cause us to do.

And what it should cause us to do is to worship the God of the universe.

The Desire

They were longing for a better country . . .

— Hebrews 11:16

My soul faints with longing for your salvation . . .

— Psalms 119:81

He has also set eternity in the hearts of men . . .

— Ecclesiastes 3:11

On this particular day, I did what I've often done many times throughout my life: I walked past the bargain section of a bookstore. Though my wallet and bank accounts have suffered greatly from this activity, I've scored many great bargains over the years, and I hoped today would be one of those days. Out of nowhere, I looked to the top shelf and saw a large coffee table book that stood out from all the others. On the cover was a bikini-wearing model. The legs and the head were conveniently removed as to draw the eyes toward the bodyscape on display. I stood looking at it for a few seconds and then I moved on. I went to the opposite end of the store. I went to the men's room. I paced. And all the while I could not get this thought out of my mind: *What does the rest of her look like?*

I'm describing one of many similar incidents I've experienced. I don't ask myself this question because of lust or sexual longings (though I have certainly allowed it to stray into those waters). I ask because I am curious. I want to understand that moment of curiosity that the female body awakens in the hearts and minds of men, a moment that can turn a man towards something stunningly beautiful or hideously evil. That curiosity we men have about Eve's form is all about an awakening of desire: the desire to see, and the desire to know.

Even while I was amid the trenches of my war with lust, I knew that women were fellow image-bearers of Christ, that they were the personification of the grace, peace, rest and sensuality of God. I knew this, but only in my mind. It was not heart knowledge, but merely a fact, a piece of information. During the war I did not look at an image of a woman's body with these thoughts in my head. From the earliest years of the war, I believed I had to avert my eyes when I saw a beautiful woman. *Eyes off, Scott. You want to look because you have a lustful heart. You're a thief. God doesn't like that. Eyes off!*

When I felt the desire to look at a woman come over me, it only made me feel worse. While it was never blunt or direct, over time I came to believe that my desire to look was lust itself. This didn't eliminate my desire. It only made it stronger. I compare this aspect of the war to the failed American experiment of Prohibition: the more off-limits you declare something, the more enticing it becomes. The minute you want to make someone addicted to something, declare that thing forbidden. It was this very subtle belief system that only made it more difficult to *stop* looking. What was even more upsetting was the underlying message that all these techniques to avoid impurity taught me: *The very second you entertain the desire to look at a woman, you are lusting. Your desire to look is lust incarnate. It is impossible to look at a woman without lusting. If you look at her, you are sinning. The only solution is to not even acknowledge the woman at all and move on.*

God took me back to the body of Eve herself to show me what was really going on with this issue of desire. I think many of us men have probably come to accept what I once thought was the truth, that we are lusting any time we want to look at a woman's body. On the surface this seems true. But when you really hold this belief under godly scrutiny, it falls apart like a teetering mountain of Jenga blocks. If I were to tell a group of men that the only way to be pure was to kill the desire to look upon the female body, I think I would receive some pretty confused looks. What man can kill his desire to look at something as beautiful as the female form? What man honestly wants to do that? What man *can* actually do that? If I told a group of women that men would never look at them again because they had to be pure, I would imagine I'd receive the same reactions. What woman wants her beauty to be ignored? God would not have made a woman's body to be the work of art it is if the only solution for male purity was to avoid looking at it. If that were so, he would be deliberately setting us up for colossal failure. That would be as unloving as God could be if it were the truth.

Two passages of Scripture help reveal what I want to share here. In the first we visit Job, the Bible's legendary man of woes. He has lost everything: possessions, family members, property, physical health. His wife criticizes him. His friends chastise him. He sits in an ash heap scraping his open sores with shards of pottery. It's a miracle in and of itself that he didn't just kill himself on the spot. In the midst of all his sorrowful soliloquies he says a curious thing: "I made a covenant with my eyes not to look lustfully at a young woman" (Job 31:1). Look again at the hopelessness of his situation. If anyone had a perfectly understandable reason for turning to lust for some sinful illusion of comfort, Job would be the man. No one would have blamed him. But even amid the worst sorrow imaginable, he says he will not do it. Our second example comes from Jesus in Matthew 5:28, where he is speaking about adultery: "But I tell you that anyone who looks at a woman lustfully has already committed adultery with her in his heart."

I had read these two passages before many times, but God showed me something new. Job does not vow to never look at a woman again. He vows to not look *lustfully*. Jesus does not say that married men cannot look at other women and appreciate their beauty after marriage. He is saying that looking at other women *lustfully* is no different than committing the act of adultery itself. Looking at a woman and looking at a woman lustfully are two completely different actions. A man who looks at artwork of the female body to feel a sense of awe, appreciation and admiration is completely different from a man who seeks out the same images to satisfy the lustful desires of his sinful nature. As Christian men, we have to understand the crucial importance of this difference, because for too long we have been led to believe that there is none. Looking at women is not our problem. It has never been our problem. Our motives behind that look and where we allow those motives to lead us is where the problem lies (more on this later).

Growing up in the church, I heard much advice about what to do to make sure that the look did not turn into lust. Yet I heard nothing about the desire itself. There was no attempt to understand it or to even address it at all. In spite of all the sermons men have heard and keep hearing about fleeing from sexual immorality, the desire to look at Eve's body remains. The act of turning our eyes away does nothing to stop this. Regardless of what we do to be pure, whether married or unmarried, our fascination with the female body never really goes away, and it never will. I don't know about you, but I would rather be lying dead in the grave than wake up one day to discover that feminine beauty no longer captivated me. I think most men would agree that the beauty of a woman's body touches a man's soul like nothing else. We are haunted by it. Given the world we live in, in all its obsessions with and exploitations of sex and female bodies, this desire appears to be a very serious dilemma for Christ-following men. But there is hope.

What God revealed to me was one of the most wonderful aspects of the freedom we can live out every day. He revealed, in a blessed simplicity, that *the desire to look at a woman's body is not sinful*. How I wish I could tell every man struggling with lust these words in person. I think this is one of the most vital and powerful messages God wants his men to know. This desire has many godly men living under a cloud of unmitigated shame. We engage in the desire to look and immediately feel bad about it. We do whatever we can to kill it. We think we have sinned, and so we self-flagellate ourselves with shame and bury our souls in guilt. I believe God is trying to tell his men that this shame is completely unnecessary.

In reality, there are few things in life that couldn't be more innocent. Think of those scenes in stories where a young boy stares in awe at a pretty girl across the room. He has never seen *anything* like this before. He has never felt his heart respond to beauty until this moment. Both of his eyes and all of his senses are widely opened. We smile in delight as we see how captivated the boy is at this gorgeous beauty whom he had never encountered before in all his life, a beauty he never knew existed. This scene is so lovely because it is so pure, so devoid of lustful corruption or evil intent, completely free of shame and guilt. *That* is what we men need to get back to, that childlike wonder of Eve that we so desperately need to reclaim. We too can gaze at the beauty of a woman's body, clothed or unclothed, and experience nothing but joy and awe.

The world tells us that we lose child-like wonder when we grow older, but we only lose it because we choose to listen to the voice of the world instead of the voice of the Artist. When we receive his glorious healing from the world, we can begin to understand and live out this desire's purity and God-given goodness. The way of innocence is not naiveté. It is one of the wisest virtues a man could ever have (Romans 16:19). What could be more freeing to know that it was God who gave us the desire to acknowledge and admire the work of his loving hands? What could be more shameful than telling men that this desire is evil?

In the same way that a desire to experience sexual intimacy is not wrong or sinful or evil, so too is it not wrong that men desire to gaze upon the glory of the female form. As God placed eternity in the hearts of men, so too did God place the desire to behold Eve's body within us. So I say to you now, man-to-man, saint-to-saint . . . do not apologize for this desire any longer. You do not have to spend another moment of your life shaming yourself for a desire that God placed in the heart of every man for a beautiful purpose. When we live in the reality of what this desire should ultimately lead us to, we can see that beholding a woman's body is something truly honorable, noble, innocent, and pure. This is especially true when we understand this desire's true foundation.

Looking back on the crop circle episode in high school, I am reminded of this running theme of beholding feminine beauty I see among men in the world today. It is commonly portrayed in coming-of-age stories. Men in these tales believe that seeing a naked woman is somehow on a par with reaching a state of tidal, full-scale nirvana. The idea of seeing her naked is often elevated to the lofty levels of a rite of passage, that it must somehow be essential to achieve manhood. Men in these tales will sometimes go to extreme lengths to see a woman without clothing, turning into voyeurs with complete disregard for their own safety, if only to see her form for a moment. A tired and well-used scene surfaces on occasion in various movies. It is always used for comedic effect and almost always with a younger man. He sees a naked woman and he says, "This is the greatest day of my life." Often the famous "Hallelujah Chorus" plays in the background, as if heaven has been reached and everything else in life will forever fail to measure up to that experience.

Many times men see a woman and think to themselves what it must be like to see her naked. Men ask women on social media to send them naked photos. Men often push women past sexual boundaries. It would be easy to just see this as sinful desire run amok. But there is far more to the desire than sin. The prevalence of this desire in the lives of men makes it clear that there is something powerful at work going on with this issue of longing to see a woman unclothed. It is the key to understanding desire itself. Not just this desire among men, but every desire the human race has ever had.

A man's desire to behold a naked woman is a desire to behold God.

Every person on Earth has felt a longing for something better. Even if it's as simple as wanting to sleep in as late as you want, or as ugly as wanting to murder your boss when he/she is being less than kind – all the things we long for, even if rooted in sin, fall under the banner of "something better." Life feels harder because that better something feels so unattainable. I once saw an article title that reminded me of this running theme of incompleteness that runs through humanity like a thread. It read: "How I Went from Being a Loser to Getting More (Sex) Than I Can Handle." Two things crossed my mind when I read the title (which was far more vulgar in reality). I thought, "Wow! What a hedonistic jerk! Thank God that's not me!" But when I seriously began thinking about it, I was shocked to discover that I'm not too different from that kid. Every time I've thought to myself, "If only . . ." that guy and I are one and the same. Not just me, but all of us. We all want what that kid wants. I would not be surprised if I ran into him today and discovered that he is still looking for nirvana. I have no difficulty imagining him enduring many sleepless nights, sleepless because he cannot escape the haunting feeling that there is *still* something better out there.

At certain times in our lives, all of us believe that once this better something is ours to have, then life will finally be what it is supposed to be. Though our world has corrupted it through lust and exploitation, the near-fanatic obsession men have with seeing women naked suddenly makes sense. We believe that when we behold a naked woman, we will finally experience something that will fulfill us. Just the sight of her will somehow fill the gaping void in our lives where contentment and happiness is supposed to exist, thereby making us whole and complete. Addicts understand this delusion full well. No matter how many times you get your fix, fulfillment will forever elude you. This is what the world has done to the female body. It has turned it into a drug.

When men put forth so much effort to take in naked women, they are not after the woman's nakedness (though they think they are). When men choose to sleep around, sex is not what they are seeking (though they think they are). It is never a quest for the drug. It is a quest for what the drug promises. Men think seeing naked women will finally bring them fulfillment without ever realizing that the beauty of a woman's body has always been intended to serve as a beacon of light towards the only One who actually possesses the ability to fulfill them forever. As Christians, when we begin to realize that what we long for in this life is true peace and lasting fulfillment, we can see right away what it is we actually long for. We long for God.

This strikes me with tremendous force. It helps me understand so many things about life. It explains every addiction on Earth. It explains adultery. It explains why we want to take vacations. It explains our longings. It explains our disappointments. We cannot grasp this war with lust without understanding that fulfillment is the sum of all we seek. Remember the law of diminishing returns? It is why men never look at only one piece of porn for the rest of their lives. It is why the sight of a single naked woman will never satisfy once and for all. The reason the law of diminishing returns has so much power is that it whispers to us in a quiet voice that there will always be something better beyond what we already have. Those verses at the start of the chapter are true of everyone whether they follow Christ or not. We all ache for eternity, and we all find ourselves seeking it in the wrong places.

As Christian men, when we nurture and invest in our relationship with Jesus and live our lives in the fullness of what he accomplished for us through the cross, we will see that there never *will* be anything better. In the same way that only Christ brings true and lasting freedom from lust, so too is he the only one who can truly fulfill us. Only he can cleanse that holy ache. The time to let him do this in our lives is now. We cannot look to the world to do it anymore. It will only continue to do what it always does. It will fail us.

There is a great scene from the movie *Cool Runnings* that always reminds me of the truth whenever I start believing the ways of the sinful nature and even the good things I desire will bring me the joy and fulfillment I want in this life. Earlier in the film, we learn that Coach Blitzer, a two-time Gold Medalist, cheated in the 1972 Winter Olympics, leading to his disqualification from the games. The incident shamed and embarrassed him for years. In all the time leading up to the final race, Derice, his lead bobsled driver, has never asked him why he did it.

– Hey Coach. I have to ask you a question. You don't have to answer if
you don't want to. I mean, I want you to, but if you can't, I understand.
– You want to know why I cheated, right?
– Yes I do.
– That's a fair question. It's quite simple, really. I had to win. You
see, Derice, I had made winning my whole life. And when you make
winning your whole life, you have to keep on winning. No matter
what. You understand that?
– No, I don't understand, Coach. You had two gold medals! You had
it all!
– Derice. A gold medal is a wonderful thing. But if you're not enough
without it, you'll never be enough with it.

We can finally see our sinful pursuits for what they are. The
instant we set out to find life apart from God, we embark on the
most dangerous and fruitless struggle the human race will ever
endure. Until we see that our obsessive longing for lasting fulfillment
can only be met by Christ, we will never be free. *The freedom, joy,
and life we can have through him can never be replaced by anything
else on Earth.* This includes the many rich blessings and good things
we have in our lives as well. Our wives, our girlfriends, the music and
movies we love, sexual intimacy in marriage, our God-given talents,
the beauty of nature, the beauty of the naked female body – these
were created to bring us happiness and joy. They were not meant
to *be* our happiness and joy. These things were designed to always
and forever point us back to the Life we truly long for so that we
might see just how wide and how vast and how unending his love
for us truly is. When we see that our many blessings are meant to
guide us to the Source of those many blessings, life can only grow
in ever-increasing richness.

I see now why this desire to behold the female body exists in
the hearts of men. It is not a corrupt desire. It is desire corrupted.
As I said earlier, when a man beholds a naked woman, he is not
beholding something to avoid at all costs. He is beholding the image
of the King of Kings. Seeing a human body is the closest we will ever
come to physically beholding God while living on this earth. Eve
is the most stunning self-portrait the world will ever know. Since

103

we cannot see God in this life, he gave us the entirety of creation and the crowning achievement of his artistic career – the female body – to reveal his indescribable grace, his powerful imagination, and his pure and romantic heart to a world that will long for it until Jesus comes again. Do we honestly think that God wants his men to ignore something that he so clearly designed to be a light that serves to illuminate him?

Lord Jesus, guide us to the right path.

Turn our desires to you that we may know you.

Open our eyes.

Open our hearts.

When we see her beauty may we see you.

May her beauty guide us to the fulfillment only you can bring.

> For everything God created is good, and *nothing is to be rejected if it is received with thanksgiving*, because it is consecrated by the word of God and prayer.
> - I Timothy 4:4-5 (emphasis added)

Life

I am a deeply romantic person. That is probably obvious to most of you by now, but it's true. I am a deeply romantic person. Though we tend to view romance as it relates to relationships with the opposite sex, romance is, to me at least, less of an emotional state and more of a way of life. As such, I try every day to remain close to the things, people and places that speak to my deep heart. Music is a huge one for me. Nature is another. Spending time in deep conversation with a friend or family member is another. I sometimes write poetry in my spare time. I read the Song of Songs fairly often. I take drives through the countryside while listening to music that touches my spirit (unlike many of my fellow Washingtonians, I love driving in the rain). My thoughts turn to the beauty of women that I see in life or in art. I say hi to my female friends with terms of affection like "Hello wonderful" or "Hello milady." Sometimes I tell them how pretty they are. I pray for my future spouse. I pray for my future marriage. I think about things I want to do with my future wife someday. I thank God for the human capacity for emotion, for love, for life. I sing praise songs to God when I go to work as a way to align myself with him. Yes, I am a romantic.

This romantic spirit of mine is not something I force. It is not born of a desire to make women attracted to me. I am not attempting to put on a show for people or fit into some cinematic "hopeless romantic" archetype. This is, to the core, who I am. It simply *is*. It is a fundamental pillar in the bedrock of my masculine identity. It is firmly grounded in my relationship with Christ, for he is the one who gave me this heart. When you are in a relationship with the one from whom all goodness and beauty flows, being romantic is no big task. Having said all this, however, I do not partake of these activities all the time. There are those I do daily and others I do on occasion. Not every encounter I have with beauty is life-altering, but it is always life-defining.

The days when I don't feel that romantic spirit are, for me at least, miserable. I don't like *not* feeling like myself. I can't stand it when I feel indifferent to life. Life tends to throw things in our way that make us feel like someone that we don't like very much. It's hard for me to deal with that aspect of the human condition. It's hard because I sometimes focus too hard on beauty. Most of the time, I just want everything to be about romance and beauty. And there lies the folly. Beauty itself can blind me to the basic truth that there is more to life than beauty. At times I can almost feel God saying to me, *I love that you love beauty, Scott. But this isn't all I have for you.* Such times remind me of how important it is to our healing from lust to simply live our lives.

A woman's beauty can draw us to worship God with all our hearts. The desire to look at a woman's body is not a sin. Now that we are armed with this freedom-giving knowledge, we must ask ourselves another question: Now that I have received the healing power of Christ, how does all of this weighty truth translate to my distraction-heavy daily existence? This is a good question to ask because, as I said before, women are everywhere. The opportunities to put these truths into action can occur daily. Now that we are free, does this mean that any woman anywhere is okay to behold? When a man sees a woman's body – clothed or unclothed, whether in art or at the beach in summer, whether it's at the grocery store or at work, intentionally or unintentionally – and he finds himself attracted, curious and fascinated, should he look on in wonder, or should he avert his eyes? What I learned was that the answer to all those questions comes down to the pivotal issue of *motive*.

In a situation like this, we must pause to ask ourselves the all-important question: Why? Why am I *really* looking at her? What am

I *really* thinking when I see her breasts, her waist, her legs, her eyes, her lips? What is the sight of this woman *really* making me want to do? Does looking at this woman make me want to have sex with her? Idolize her? Worship God? Now that I know that my desire to look at her body is an extension of a desire for God, is it truly his beauty I want to see or not? How we answer these questions means everything.

Think back to the man faced with temptation at his computer. Just as it was with him, so it is with us in such moments. There are two outcomes. If the sight of a woman's body causes us to marvel in wonder at our God and draws you close to him, if we invite him into the experience of beholding her beauty – if it makes us *worship* him – there is no sin in it. When we want to look at a woman's body, we should be doing so with this mindset: "I want to marvel at the work of God's hands. I want to look at something that guides me to the Artist who created beauty in the first place. I want to experience a vision of the one who will truly and forever fulfill me." However, if the opposite is happening, then all the advice for purity the church has supported and upheld through the years must be followed. If we find that all we are drawn to is sexual fantasy, idolatry, dwelling only on our pleasure – turning back to the ways of the sinful nature from which Christ died to set us free – then we must look away. No exceptions. We must look away.

Glorious freedom from the scourge of lust is ours to have. It has always been ours to have. But after all I have stated about how the beauty of the female body should draw us closer to God and away from ourselves, it is vitally important that we remember I Peter 2:16:

> Live as free men, but do not use your freedom as
> a cover-up for evil. Live as servants of God.

This verse is so helpful because it is such a great reminder of what our freedom *isn't*. We cannot use our freedom in Christ as an insurance policy or a good luck charm. Our freedom cannot be a tool we use to convince ourselves that we can continue to resume our lives in service to the sinful nature. I did something similar to this in the course of the war. Many times I gazed at women and tried to convince myself that I was looking because I just wanted to look for the sake of looking. I did not want to dishonor these women. I did not want to lust. I just wanted to look. The women were pretty, so why not? Every single time I did that, it turned into the passionate lust of the heathen. Not once or twice. Every time. Why? Because my motives were not pure from the very beginning. Instead of being honest with myself and turning away, I tried to use innocent motives to justify my sinful desires. I believed that I could make myself see women correctly through my own strength of will. I was wrong.

The whole goal of our freedom from lust should be a stronger and ever-growing relationship with Christ, not to give us license to look at any woman we want. If we are truly serious about being set free, we must seek God's wisdom on what is acceptable for us and what is not. I believe this looks different for all of us (see Romans 14).

I'll use myself as an example to illustrate what I mean. One of my personal rules with my female friends is that I won't go over to her house or apartment if she's all by herself, and I won't invite her over if I'm alone at my place. I'm not worried that my friend will seduce me. I'm not worried that I will force her beyond her boundaries. I have this rule because I will not allow an environment for passion to ignite, no matter how unlikely it seems. Logic and passion are like oil and water. I've read too many stories of godly Christian couples or friends who put themselves in a situation like this. There was never an ounce of sinful intent from either person. The thought was, "We're Christians. This can't happen. This won't happen." But one of them gave the other a look. One of them put some music on. There was maybe some deep conversation or even prayer. Before long, they let passion consume them, and the only remnant from that moment of passion was a destroyed relationship. As far as I'm concerned, I don't want to test whether I have the zeal to resist this passion. It's too dangerous for me.

Now, for other men, this situation could be completely harmless.

There could be no temptation whatsoever to go down into darkness. I've committed to not put myself or a woman in that position, but not every man has to do the same because not all men are tempted the same. This applies to portrayals of feminine beauty. A man could be drawn to God by an image of a woman that would lead another man astray. It is pivotal to our purity that we seek God's wisdom on this issue while keeping the words of I Corinthians 10:31 firmly before us: "Whatever you do, do it all for the glory of God."

If you choose to not so much as enter a magazine aisle in a store because you believe it would not be right for you, I am all for it. If you choose to take up figure drawing or art classes because you know you can do so and be pure before God, I'm all for it. A man who can admire artworks of the female nude with godly motives is no less pure than a man who avoids anything resembling bare flesh. What we must remember is this: *What you believe is acceptable for you is between you and God.* You do not need man's approval or permission to seek something that truly draws you closer to him. The reverse to this is that we cannot declare what is acceptable in our own lives as immediately acceptable to others. *I* certainly don't want to do this. After all I've said about nudity not being evil and how not all images of nudity are evil and that the act of beholding it is not evil, the last thing on Earth I want is for what I said to be taken as me saying that you can now go ahead and look at nudity all you want. Scott J. Einig is not exactly a qualified stand-in for God. It is God alone who has the verdict on what is appropriate for his men as individuals to take in with their eyes.

However, in light of this issue of what is acceptable and what is not, there are sights and situations that we simply have to avoid at all costs. Not just me. Everyone. Here is how we define what those things may be: Anything that exists to exploit, defile or insult a woman's beauty or any image that is intended sorely for a man's sexual arousal is out of bounds. Pornography is the best example. Espresso stands with bikini-clad baristas are another. Advertisements geared toward men that use women to help sell their products are another. While it is true that a woman's physical beauty is still present in these things, it is not being used to draw men to praise and honor that beauty, let alone to praise and honor the Artist who gave it to us in the first place. These things do not teach us anything about female beauty that is true and right, therefore they have no place in our lives. It's as simple as that. Such things have the power to draw us back into the corruption of the world and make the light of God's truth diminish.

Sex in movies and television is another example that must be brought to light. I have been an ardent lover of cinema for almost all my life (what the more literate would call a cinephile). Naturally, I've come across a fair share of onscreen sex. This was a mighty and bloody battlefield for me during the war. To this day, my largest struggle with lust involves trying to overcome various memories of certain sex scenes. Most Christians would say that all sex in the movies is bad, but I do not agree. Though extremely rare in our world today, there *are* some films that treat human sexuality with respect and honesty. Not all sex scenes exploit and demean a woman's beauty, but the sad truth is that almost all screen sex is either intended to arouse an audience, make them uncomfortable, or make them point their fingers and laugh. For a man trying to be sexually pure for the name of Christ, this is something that has to go. We have nothing of value to learn from it.

Along with TV and movies, music is another thing we must be cautious about. The danger with music is that because the beats and the rhythms are so catchy, we rarely pause and actually listen to or even think about the meaning of the lyrics we are singing. Picture a demon whispering something in your ear that sounds really good over and over again until you begin repeating the same thing out loud, and you can paint a good picture of the effect of a lot of music in the world (it was Lucifer himself, after all, who composed music in heaven before his fall). There are vile lyrics out there that accomplish through song what porn does through imagery. It doesn't matter how innocent and romantic it all sounds or how the world views it. God's men should not be shouting and singing the rhythmic anthems of a sick society.

There are certain women we cannot be around. Some women are like the adulteress spoken of in Proverbs 5, 6 and 7 (interesting that there are three chapters devoted to warning us against such women. It appears that God thought it was pretty important). There are women who will do almost anything to get the attention and intimacy of men, women who will use their beauty and their bodies as instruments of seduction:

> For the lips of the adulterous woman drip honey,
>   and her speech is smoother than oil;
>   but in the end she is bitter as gall,
>   sharp as a double-edged sword.
> Her feet go down to death;
>   her steps lead straight to the grave.
> She gives no thought to the way of life;
>   her paths wander aimlessly, but she does not know it.
> Now then, my sons, listen to me;
>   do not turn aside from what I say.
> Keep to a path far from her,
>   do not go near the door of her house . . .
>   – Proverbs 5:3-8

> I find more bitter than death
>   the woman who is a snare,
>   whose heart is a trap
> and whose hands are in chains.
> The man who pleases God will escape her
>   but the sinner she will ensnare.
>   – Ecclesiastes 7:26

David's story in II Samuel 11 is a graphic example of what happens when a righteous man allows unrighteous infatuation to take a foothold. He saw Bathsheba bathing on the roof, and all of a sudden nothing else mattered. All those psalms and feats of victory over his enemies suddenly had no impact on his life. In that moment this unknown woman (already married, I might add) became the only thing he cared about. Bathsheba's captivating, God-created beauty did not draw David to the Artist but to himself. Suddenly his fulfillment was no longer found in God, but in this incredibly beautiful woman who he didn't even know. I think the debate about whether Bathsheba seduced David or not is irrelevant. The point is that she was put in a position she never should have been put in. Had David acted in honor the moment his eyes first saw her, so much terrible pain could have been avoided. Had he seen her on the roof, given thanks to God for her awe-inspiring beauty and not given a moment's thought as to how he could gratify the temptation of lustful desire, the following tragedies would have never occurred.

Joseph's story in Genesis 39 provides the best example possible for what to do when encountering a woman who displays the attributes of the adulteress: run. This is not a simple biblical anecdote. It's what a man actually has to do. If a woman dishonors her body in a way that encourages men to do the same, we must have nothing to do with her, nor should we associate ourselves with those who indulge in and support such behavior. Our world calls this "being judgmental." God calls it wisdom. It is scary how easy it is to disregard morals, standards and beliefs for a seductress who promises pleasure. God's Word tells us time and again that such pursuits are absolutely not worth it. History itself reminds us over and over that it is not worth it. As a result of his choice to remain pure, Joseph was thrown in prison for over two years. He also ended up ruling Egypt alongside Pharaoh. How did such good fortune happen? Because Joseph knew that making a stand for God was worth the pain of sacrifice, and God never leaves nor forsakes those who follow him.

This resistance to Satan's perversions of female beauty that can grow in a man comes from aligning ourselves with God through prayer, action, and relationship. The more a man grows in the ability to see through the Artist's eyes, the more he will see the sirens for what they are and the less he will want to answer their wayward call. When a man's desires are God's desires, he will not be so easily manipulated by evil portrayals of female beauty. Though we may not feel or receive any earthly rewards for making a stand for righteousness, be encouraged to know that our stands will reap rewards in eternity. Remember, men, that as sons of God, you and I are foreigners while we live on Earth. Our citizenship is heaven.

Our greatest rewards should never be staked on this life. That's the world's way of thinking. The world says, "This life is all you have, so do whatever it takes to enjoy it!" To those people God says, "Woe to you." God sees your righteous deeds, and he is well-pleased. Earthly pleasures fade into shadows and dust. Our eternal rewards will never end. Ephesians 5:8-14 sums up all that I am saying wonderfully (emphasis added):

> For you were once darkness, but now you are light in the Lord. Live as children of light (for the fruit of the light consists in all goodness, righteousness and truth) and find out what pleases the Lord. *Have nothing to do with the fruitless deeds of darkness, but rather expose them.* For it is shameful even to mention what the disobedient do in secret. But everything exposed by the light becomes visible—and everything that is illuminated becomes a light.

Even though God guided me into the life of freedom I live in now, I have had temptations in my day-to-day life that have truly tested me. I won't pretend that I've never had the intense desire to go back and look at the same porn and sex scenes that held me captive during the war. For me, the mental battle is far more difficult than the physical. I won't pretend that I haven't stumbled. There have been moments when I've wanted to look at women for impure reasons. I experienced such an episode not too long ago.

I was driving home from work and decided to swing by an espresso. I pulled up to the window, and the good-looking barista opened it to take my order. Let's just say that she was wearing a shirt that clearly defined the size and contour of her breasts. Outwardly I showed no sign of discomfort or awkwardness, but inside, my heart was going, "Wow!" I ordered my coffee, she and I had a very pleasant chat about the upcoming Christmas season, and I drove away. I was still in a state of mild shock at how unexpected the whole encounter was. Being faced with the beauty of the female body so suddenly has a way of catching me off guard. Lust was not at all present in this incident. The desire to lust was not present in that moment or afterward. I did not have any kind of sexual response. But nonetheless, I was thrilled. There is no denying that beholding a woman's body can be thrilling. I thanked God for her captivating beauty. I drove home. Life went on.

A month or so later, I was on my way to work, and I thought about going to that same coffee stand again. Now, I live in the Pacific Northwest near Seattle, Washington. Coffee stands are not exactly scarce. The highway I was driving on had at least five other stands I could have gone to. But I wanted to go back to that specific stand. I found myself going through a whole list of reasons to do so. *It's on my way to work. I have time. Maybe she'll be there and we can chat again. She was a good conversationalist. She was years older than me. It's not like I want to date her or anything. I thought my drink was really tasty last time. The prices were fair. All I want to do is see if she's there so we can chat. The prices were fair, weren't they?* On and on my mental list went. The only thing I didn't add to my little list was the real reason I wanted to go back. What I really wanted was to see her breasts again. After all this bargaining and justifying, I finally decided to be honest with myself. *My motives for going to that stand are not pure or good. I know I'm better than that. God created me to be better than that. I can't do this.* I drifted back to the right lane. I was approaching the stand. A semi was up ahead of me in the left lane. I sped up next to it so that I wouldn't be able to see the stand as I drove by. I like to think that God provided that semi for me.

This is one incident of many. I have had numerous times when I've wanted to look at women who are clearly not using the beauty of their bodies for good reasons. As Paul said when describing the sinful nature, I can sometimes feel the spirit of impurity standing there with me. And so I turn away. Sometimes I'm looking at a woman and I begin to thank God and honestly worship him, but lustful thoughts and memories come in to try to pervert my time of praise, and so I rebuke the enemy and turn away. By checking my heart and walking away if I sense impurity, lust has no chance of coming back. When Satan tries to fight, I fight back. In the course of the war I rarely chose to do this, because I was in devoted service to my sinful desires. As I said, the more you seek Christ, the more your motives will be set on the path of holiness. I find it significantly easier to turn away from exploited women when I am walking with the Artist.

Sometimes an opposite situation happens, something that leaves me in awe of the heart of my King. There will be days where I am walking along, living my life, when suddenly my eyes fall on a woman's body – in person, a magazine cover, an article, a book – and I find something odd happening. I find myself unable to look. Not because of lust, but because of the sheer power of her beauty. This has occurred to me through the simplest of situations. One time I was in church and one of the women a few rows in front of me tied her hair up. As I watched her do this I found myself deeply moved. The way her hands moved through her hair, the grace in which she performed this simple act, touched something in me. I watched her for a while and then I had to turn my head away. Here's another example. As working-class adults, sometimes our jobs entail long hours of sitting or standing. After doing this for a long time you need to stretch to get some of that lost life back. I see women do this on occasion, just stretching to regain that long-lost limberness. On the surface this is no big thing. Every person does this. But whenever I see a woman stretch, I feel something in my heart begin to stir. Something inside at the soul level awakens. With these various encounters comes a sense of longing so tangible that it goes beyond a mere emotional response and becomes an ache I can physically feel. It is not for the woman herself, but for *something*. For beauty. For eternity.

These situations remind me of a profound truth. Sometimes beauty is hard to look at *because* it is so beautiful. It hurts. It goes like an arrow to the most vulnerable places of the soul. I feel that I am not worthy of beholding it. Having the relationship with Christ that I do, I am blessed with the knowledge of knowing the one who is orchestrating these encounters. It's his way of saying, *This is my heart. This is my beauty. See what I have made. Come to me.* There is no greater reminder of God's sensuality, grace, rest, peace and beauty than the female form. As I have said before and will not get tired of saying, a woman's body has this level of power because that is exactly how God made it. God uses these incredibly deep encounters with feminine beauty to remind me that, as his beloved son who has been set free from the law of sin and death, I am able to look in awe, free of shame, and allow my soul to be touched by the work of his hands. He says through Eve's beauty, *This is who I am*. In times like that, God and I are as close as marriage partners at the altar.

As we live our lives and apply all these things to the way we live, I believe there are three things we must *not* do to make these things a reality: We must not try to kill the desire to look at Eve's body, we must not linger on her form to the point of worshiping the creation, and we must not give lust an iota of room to grow within us. If we look at a woman's body and choose to be honest about our motives, we must do the right thing. It is all the more important to do what is righteous because *God knows what we're up to*. A man can lie to himself and say, "I'm only looking for the sake of looking because it's normal and no one cares and that's just how men are, deal with it." A man can use the most poetic language imaginable to make people think he actually values a woman's beauty when all he cares about is the lustful pleasure it brings him. A man can live his entire life without anyone knowing what he really values about women. But if there is one thing he should never stop believing, it's this: He cannot thwart God.

Jesus provides the best example of living out this truth. When he was fasting in the desert and tempted by the devil three times, he was alone. No other witnesses were present to see these trials. Had he given in to the devil, no one on Earth would have known about it. But Jesus knew the reality. His Father would have known. He resisted Satan's temptations for the sake of his Heavenly Father, because Jesus knew that it was the eyes and heart of his Father that mattered most. So let me say it again. You can try to justify your sin all you want. But you cannot thwart God.

> . . . serve him with wholehearted devotion
> and with a willing mind, for the Lord searches every heart
> and understands every desire and every thought (I Chronicles 28:9).

> Does he not see my ways
> and count my every step (Job 31:4)?

> You have set our iniquities before you,
> our secret sins in the light of your presence (Psalm 90:8).

> For your ways are in full view of the LORD,
> and he examines all your paths (Proverbs 5:21).

> The eyes of the LORD are everywhere,
> keeping watch on the wicked and the good (Proverbs 15:3).

> There is no wisdom, no insight, no plan
> that can succeed against the LORD (Proverbs 21:30).

> All a man's ways seem innocent to him,
> but motives are weighed by the Lord (Proverbs 16:2).

> For God will bring every deed into judgment,
> including every hidden thing, whether
> it is good or evil (Ecclesiastes 12:14).

> Woe to those who go to great depths
> to hide their plans from the Lord,
> who do their work in darkness and think,
> "Who sees us? Who will know?" (Isaiah 29:15).

> Who can hide in secret places so that I
> cannot see them?" declares the Lord.
> "Do not I fill heaven and earth?"
> declares the Lord (Jeremiah 23:24).

> What we are is plain to God, and I hope
> it is also plain to your conscience (II Corinthians 5:11).

These verses are not in the Bible to scare you. They are there to guide your steps toward the path of righteousness. The world says, "Men just can't help it!" The Lord says, "Be holy, because I am holy" (Leviticus 11:44). Though the voice of the world is powerful and the ways of the world seem right, it is nothing but a clever counterfeit of the freedom-giving life God offers us. The call to a life of holiness and sexual purity is something we can answer through Christ in us. Seek his ways and his will and eradicate lust from your life. Come to see women through God's eyes. Your life will change in ways too wonderful for words.

The female form is powerful and dangerous.

It has the power to lead us to life or to death.

May God open your eyes and your hearts through her beauty.

May God use her beauty to move you to worship him like never before.

May he lead you to life everlasting.

Sex & Marriage

The Pacific Northwest has a fantastically accurate reputation for rainfall (it's raining right now as I write this). I can say with honesty that if you live there, you're going to get trainloads of rain during certain times of the year. I live next to a valley, and during flood season the valley fills with water like a bathtub. One night when I was fourteen or fifteen, I decided to take a walk to see the recent flood up close. It was a beautiful night, very clear and alive. I walked to the section of road where the floodwater had covered it. I didn't just go outside to see some cool-looking storm residue. I went out there with a troubled soul, needing to have a question answered. After a while, I asked God to tell me who I was. He told me something in a voice that went right into my soul and has stayed there ever since: *You are my beloved son.* Since that night, those words have been the cornerstone of my identity. I knew who I was and who I belonged to. *I am God's son, and he is my Father.* God instilled that foundation firmly in me from that point onward.

You may recall in Part I that I never gave in to lust for reasons of masculine validation. The twelve-year war for my heart had nothing to do with an ill-fated search for my identity as a man. For many men, this is why lust is so prevalent in their lives. They want to know who they are and so they turn to something other than God that gives them something resembling an answer. It wasn't that way with me. I did not lust because I wanted to feel like a man.

I lusted because I wanted sex.

I wanted to actually experience the act itself.

I wanted fulfillment.

119

Though I myself am a virgin, I know about sex. Because it is one of the deepest desires of my heart, I have done more than my fair share of knowledge-seeking. I had two deeply influential mentors that taught me about the subject. One was the world. The other was God. The first mentor led me on paths that seemed straight and true but proved to be fraught with death and hopelessness. Where the first mentor proved itself nothing more than a desolate fraud, the second mentor guided me to truth, and ultimately, hope.

Now that I can look back over the war and see more clearly where I was led astray, I can also see where God has replaced lies with truth and ultimately healed and restored my beliefs about his gift of sex. He has done this for me over the years by leading me to the written and spoken words of others. God has guided me to many honest sources about marriage and sex, in which many stories are shared and much valuable wisdom given. I've also been fortunate to have many people throughout my life who have been willing to discuss the topic of sex with me. I owe a lot of this chapter to the wisdom and honesty of others, and for them I am very grateful.

I can't remember exactly when my own sexual desire began, but if one were to ask, I would say it awoke around the time the war had been going on for a few years. When the war began I simply wanted to gaze lustfully at naked women. As I progressed further into the notoriously awkward journey of puberty, sexual desire eventually came into my experience of taking in the female body. Because I have always placed physical sex within the non-negotiable moral borders of marriage, I decided to take the coward's route. I gazed at and masturbated to sex scenes in movies, porn and naked pictures in complete isolation and safety from anyone's knowledge. I would not physically engage with a woman, so I picked the nearest thing to it I could get.

This desire to experience sexual intimacy was, in my opinion, the largest reason I struggled for so long. Like many others, I thought that if I could only get married and have an active sex life, lust would not be a problem. Thankfully, God opened my eyes to the dual reality that the purpose of marriage is not to provide me with sex whenever I want it, and that when it comes to killing lust in my life, marriage is not the solution. These truths became especially important to me after that wonderful period of reading Gardner's book. Now that I knew the godly purpose of sex in marriage, my desire for it increased, though with holy intent.

However, this did not last. Rather than going away, my lust still persisted. Overtime, sex and the desire to experience it became monumental idols in my life. I fell into the mindset of a kid wanting ice cream when a plate of healthy greens is shoved into his face. I found myself asking God questions with that same level of maturity. My rants to God looked something like this: "God, why can't this be for me? I desire sex for holy reasons. And here I am, still single and still not experiencing this gift. Why does sex seem to be this wonderful thing that everyone else in the world seems to be enjoying? A lot of those people aren't even following you, Jesus! So here I am, a son of God who loves you with all his heart, not getting to experience this. What the heck? Why can't you bring me a spouse so I can start enjoying this already?"

How I would love to say that I never feel this way anymore. Though my desire has become far healthier, holier, and far more realistic than what it once was, I would be a liar if I said I did not sometimes experience the feeling of being left out of a wonderful party that I was somehow not invited to. Thankfully, our God is a God of grace and mercy. When I feel the need to lament to God that I'm *still* not experiencing the gifts of marriage and sex, he continually gives me hope. However imperfectly, I am learning how to claim that hope for myself, to say every day with assurance, "God, you are faithful." But during the war for my heart, I was sorely lacking in hope. In the heat of my frustration and shame, this what-about-me attitude was practically my motto. And it was one of the reasons why I continually chose to lust in spite of all that God revealed to me.

Satan knows full well that sex is possibly the easiest thing in the world to idolize. I don't need to list the overwhelming evidence of that fact. Every day, we hear and read supposedly "new" and "groundbreaking" and "pleasure-enhancing" news about how we can make our sex lives better. It sends the message that if we don't somehow experience sex according to the world's standards (or experience sex at all), then we must have pretty god-awful lives. And we have been tricked into believing this lie. *Our* experience, *our* pleasure, *our* orgasm, *our* sensations. It is what *we* get out of it that matters most. If *we* are not the ones experiencing the greatest sex imaginable, we need to do whatever it takes to make sure we do. In the blinding fog of lust, the truth doesn't matter. We blindfold our souls with the cloth of selfishness.

In this whole sinful process we are creating a biological sex drive that eventually has the power to control us as opposed to the other way around. It happened to me all throughout the war. The more I lustfully sought and the more I masturbated, the more and more a mere glance at a woman made me want to turn back to the sex scenes or porn videos and feed the sex drive I had allowed to run amok. This is what makes those hormone fires so incredibly difficult to put out. Our bodies are sexually responding to this out-of-control urge that we have let out of the cage. And, as with so many actions that cause self-destruction, we do whatever we can to justify it.

Human biology tells us about the male body's natural buildup of semen and how the body needs to release said buildup after a few days. This is true. Therefore, we use biological facts as an excuse of *needing* release to justify our lust. Looking at sex as a purely biological act is something the world tells us to do all the time. The world brings sex down to the base level of a bodily function, trying to tell us not to worry about or get emotional about it because it's "just sex." Another especially troubling message that men are assaulted by on a daily basis is that they need sex to be men. The world turns the act of sexual intercourse into the doorway to true manhood, telling us that it is vital to actually being a man at all. *Real* men get it all the time! All you have to do is conquer a woman sexually and you've made it!

For so many of us, when it comes to sex, this is our reality. But as sons who belong to the Artist, you and I know there is a better way. Honoring Eve and seeing her body with the eyes of God is what makes us men. No man or woman on this earth *needs* sex and orgasm to survive. We can be the men God calls us to be without them. We cannot kill our sex drive, but we have the ability to keep it under control. That includes you. That includes me. It's time we made *this* our reality. The enemy has fed us lies like candy bars with razor blades shoved inside, and we have been gobbling it up and slicing our mouths open with reckless abandon. How wonderful to know that we serve the One who can mend our broken views of his sacred gifts!

In order to have our minds cleansed of the world's poison, we must go back to the truth of what sex is. In the same way that we must look at feminine beauty with God's eyes, we must do the same with sex. In the eyes of God, sex is inseparable from marriage. One cannot be fully had without the other. It has been this way from the beginning. This means we must understand God's intent for marriage to fully grasp God's intent for sex. Most of the time I don't want to put forth the effort to do this. During the war there were countless times when I became angry for having to wait to be married to have sex (I know I'm not alone here). But that was because I was selfishly ignoring vital truths. One of the largest of those truths is that marriage is a sacred covenant.

We see this demonstrated in the Old Testament many times. God binds himself to one of his servants through a covenant that carries through to future generations. These covenants are not limited to words. They are not true covenants without some form of binding action. The vows are spoken first, and then the two members do something as a way of physically carrying it out. Whether it is building a monument or changing a lifestyle or leaving a visible scar on the body, something physical must happen to seal the covenant.

In the case of a marriage covenant, sex is that physical action, the ritual that serves as the divine covenant seal. The spoken vow says, "I will enjoy and desire sexual intimacy with you and you alone." The covenant is laid out and sworn before God and man, and then the door is opened to physically fulfilling that holy promise through the gift of sexual intimacy. Having this covenant mindset of sex and marriage makes us see why affairs are so devastating. Marital unfaithfulness is a far bigger issue than "I did something I shouldn't have done." Infidelity says, "The oaths I made to be sexually attracted to you alone don't matter to me anymore." An affair takes the beauty of binding yourself to one another through a holy covenant and completely destroys it. Is it any wonder why the Bible would speak so frequently about the dangers of adultery, or why the Word states explicitly that God hates divorce?

Looking at sex in this light can go a long way in helping us understand why God created it to be saved for marriage. But that never stopped me from believing there was more to it than that. I still wondered, sometimes obsessively, why God designed it like this. Sex is such a powerful force, so why did God make it his plan to keep sex exclusively in the boundaries of the marriage bed? We fallen humans sure seem to be tempted by it a lot, so why did his plan not allow us to engage in sex with no strings attached? Not surprisingly, the answer leads back to our Savior. When we accept Jesus into our hearts, we are entering the spiritual equivalent of a marriage relationship. We bind ourselves to God for eternity. Like a physical earthly marriage, it is a union that man should not destroy. Over and over again in the Bible, God uses marriage as a metaphor for the kind of relationship and the kind of love he has for us. God's love for his people is nothing if not *fierce*. For us as individuals, our marriage union to Christ is supposed to only grow more intense and more passionate until death unites us forever in eternity. The love we share with Christ in this spiritual marriage should never stop growing stronger in romance, selflessness, sacrifice and joy.

So where does sex fit into this? One of the most mysterious and profound purposes God created sex for was to illustrate how vast and how good his romance, selflessness, sacrifice and joy – his married love – with us truly is. Sexual intimacy is the earthly representation of that fierce love God has for his people, what we call the church. When I first learned this, it blew me away, because I thought, "Wow, God! If sex is just a *representation* of your love for us, then how much more pleasurable will that love be when you take us home!" The Old Testament portrays endless examples of God's heart pouring out to Israel as only a wounded lover can. We see firsthand how heartbreaking it is to watch God's people continue in their infidelity. Yet in spite of all the ways the church wounds the heart of God, he never asks for a divorce. He only redoubles his efforts to make that love more tangible and more real. That's the beauty of covenant love. It does not bail out when the tempest strikes. It is solid as the roots of the mountains. It is faithful. It is eternal.

As image-bearers of God, when a married man and woman engage in sexual intimacy, they are living out and recreating the representation of that fiery, soul-touching love. Sex is God's way of saying to his people, "This is how I feel about you." Or as the Word says in Jeremiah 31:3, "I have loved you with an everlasting love." That's quite a love, is it not?

I now see why God intended to keep sex inside marriage and marriage alone, and why we as God's men must honor his design. Sex is an illustration of the kind of love that cannot exist apart from eternal covenant. Apart from marriage, sex can never be what God designed it to be. Apart from marriage, it is and always will be second best, a clever forgery instead of the true and authentic original. We must cling to this, men. We must not allow ourselves to forget this, because the world will always tell us otherwise.

When we actively rage against the world's godless representations of sex, we can also see something essential to God-ordained sexual intimacy that the world keeps chasing after and will never discover: God designed sex to fulfill us. Looking back over my sinful wanderings, I can now see how I tried in vain to fill the vacant place in my heart that sexual intimacy with my future mate will one day occupy. I didn't allow God to fill that empty place, so I chose lust. I never left from masturbating to an image of a woman with a deep sense of fulfillment. I always had to have more because it was never enough. It was the law of diminishing returns reborn as a lifestyle of broken promises. Lust promised fulfillment, and never once did I receive any. What I *did* receive was emptiness, loneliness, shame, doubt and guilt (things sexual intimacy was created to destroy). When God made sex, he created it to not only bring him honor, but to fill our hearts and souls with the fruit of the Spirit. When a husband and wife engage in that glorious unity according to God's standards – seeking not only pleasure for themselves but for each other – there will be a deep knowledge that they have fulfilled each other's needs and touched each other's hearts. Husbands and wives need an entire lifetime to discover the ways in which they may sacrificially fulfill one another. Love is sacrifice. God knows this better than we ever will.

This is why he created marriage and sex to be inseparable. This is why he created marriage and sex to act as holy ambassadors for his people to show what his love for us really looks like. And so I ask:

Why would any follower of Christ want less than this?

Do we honestly want second-best to be our standard?

Is that what God wants for us?

Now that we've discussed God's plan and purpose for sex, I must now bring up the issue of masturbation. Any time sex is the topic of conversation, masturbation is inevitably brought into the discussion. There is really no getting around it. And that's okay. It should not be an elephant in the room. More importantly, it should not be ignored. For my own part, one can look at my story and draw his or her own conclusions as to how we must treat masturbation. As I discussed earlier about the issue of beholding nudity, masturbation is viewed by many as an absolute sin. No way could it be anything else. But after having received sexual healing from God, I want to present a rethinking of this issue that has so many of us confused, upset, and ashamed.

One only has to look at the word "masturbation," and instantly there is some kind of strong reaction. For most of us, this reaction is a negative one. It makes sense. All we have to do is look at our own stories and recall the kind of mental and moral destruction that masturbation is capable of causing. But instead of only looking at masturbation as A Sin, I want us to look closer to see if this is actually the truth. One man I spoke with explained it this way: the Bible is very clear about what is sin. Drunkenness, murder, adultery, foul language, idolatry, stealing, lying, greed, lust . . . there is no argument about whether these are sins or not. The fact that masturbation is not mentioned in the Bible at all makes a strong case for it *not* being a sin. Masturbation can be born of sin, but it is not sin in and of itself.

I've heard some people call masturbation "lust in action," and in some cases it is. This is the kind of masturbation I did all throughout the war. If a man sees an actual woman he is not married to and uses her for sexual gratification, that is adultery of the heart (Matthew 5:28). Having said this, a man who masturbates because he wants to experience the physical pleasure of orgasm is different than a man who masturbates while imagining himself having sex with a real woman. It can be done without lusting after an actual woman mentally or physically. I believe masturbation is something that can be done purely in the same way that drinking a beer or smoking a cigarette can be done purely. A man may do these things because he enjoys them on occasion, or he may be doing them obsessively because of unresolved heart issues. And as we talked about earlier, if we don't guard our hearts, we can end up swimming in some mighty dangerous waters.

While it is true that a man can never once have sexual release in his life and still live to tell about it, that drive is still there. I admit that sometimes this drives me crazy. Sometimes I wish that I could just turn it off until I get married. But since we can't do that, then what's a man to do? I believe we must do three things if we want to handle our sex drives well: We should embrace it, learn about it, and learn how we can use it with wisdom. Unless lust or abuse of the sex drive is involved, I don't believe a man is sinning by giving himself release. We cannot kill the sex drive. But we *can* and *should* control it. If we choose to be honest with ourselves, we will know whether we are using it for sin or not. It has been helpful for me to ask myself these questions: *What is actually fueling my desire for sexual release? Is it my body or is it my lust? Have I managed to keep my sex drive under control or have I turned it into an idol?*

Masturbation is no different than what I stated about looking at the female form. For some men, it may be something that they can do purely before the Lord. For others, it may be a direct path to sin. You know your histories, men. You know which paths tempt you the most. This is why you and you alone have to be the one to go before God and honestly seek out his answers for you in this area. As it is with taking in the sight of the female form, it is a boundary that can only be worked out between you and God. You know why you want to look at feminine beauty. And you also know why you want to masturbate. I think these questions are the ultimate way to test our freedom as followers of Christ: "Is this drawing me closer to God or driving me away from him? Is this adding to my brokenness or helping me grow in wholeness? Is this interfering with my intimacy with Christ, or is this helping me grow in that intimacy?" When it comes to this issue and every other issue about our lives, we must come to know the answers for ourselves. We will remain incomplete until we do.

Though I do not believe masturbation is in and of itself a sin, I believe we can grow immensely in character by denying it. When we look at God's design for sex, one thing stands out: It was never intended to be a solo act. It is about a married man and woman becoming one and learning how to meet each other's sexual desires out of their selfless love for one another as they live out a shared life in marriage. When it came to the issue of a married couple's sex life, I used to believe some things about it that may seem familiar: They can have it any time they want. Both mates will have sex drives completely in sync. Every sexual encounter will be fulfilling, effortless, perfect, and filled with an endless supply of simultaneous orgasms. It was a gradual shock to me when I learned from others that these things could not be further from the truth.

Sex is just as much about a wife's fulfillment as it is about a husband's. A woman's sex drive is far different from a man's. Fulfilling sex takes work. She doesn't always want it. Sometimes she wants it when he doesn't. She may like something sexually that he doesn't. Sex can be easy to receive and also extremely difficult to give. It has the potential to be a garden or a battleground. It can make a marriage beautiful or end it altogether. This does not sound like the Elysian paradise virgins like me sometimes believe sexual encounters are every single time. Whether we can accept it or not, this is the honest reality of a sex life in marriage. Masturbation does not successfully teach us this reality. Rather, it teaches us to grow accustomed to receiving pleasure whenever the urge moves us.

Marriage and sex were designed by God to help us learn the art of selfless love. When we marry, there are times when we must deny our own desires for the sake of the one we love, and that includes the area of sexual desire. Even if we can do it and be pure before God, masturbation ultimately does not help us grow in the virtue of selfless denial. In the end, it is always about *our* pleasure. Whether we want it to be or not, it always ends up being about us. Always. It is for these reasons that I do not speak very highly of masturbation. Sure, we may be able to do it free of sin, but you will never catch me encouraging anyone to do it. When all is said and done, I would place masturbation in the same category as fast food. It tastes incredible. Eating it will not send you to hell. The desire to eat it is not an evil desire. But at the end of the day, even if your heart, feelings and mentality towards fast food are all in the right place, it really isn't all that good for you.

Out of all the wise words I've received from married people, one piece of wisdom always stands out to me: Sex and orgasm is so pleasurable because it is *shared*. Sex is something you do *with* someone. Orgasm is had *through* someone. That someone is your wife, the woman you chose above all others to unite with in marriage, the one that God set apart to be with you in the trials and beauties of life. An orgasm provided by your spouse has great potential for ushering in that special, one-of-a-kind oneness that cannot be had with anyone else. An orgasm provided by masturbation will feel great for a minute, and then you're not really left with much. When you masturbate, you can never experience the beauty of fulfilling another person.

Hearing things like this gives me a zeal to stop serving myself sexually. We serve a God who wants the best for his sons and daughters, and masturbation isn't it. When I really look at the desires of my heart, I don't want to experience the ultimate human pleasure alone. It is a source of tremendous joy that I want my future mate to be a part of. I want to grow in denying what *I* want as a way to honor and serve my future mate in the marriage bed. Sexual self-denial can be a tool to help prepare me. Am I perfect in this? No. But the desire to do so is still strong. In denying masturbation, we can learn a better way. When it comes to sex, I want what everyone wants: the best. That can only occur by honoring and following God's design.

Marriage and sex.

No matter what the world shouts, claims as absolute fact, and declares from the rooftops, the two cannot exist in their absolute best without one another. Throughout history mankind has tried in desperate futility to separate the two. Look back over my story or the stories of countless others to see how well it has worked. Brothers, whether we are married or single, the pleasure of sex is a holy gift that we must honor and respect with our bodies and our lives by making sure it *stays* set apart in the sacrament of marriage. Yes, as human beings we have sexual desires, but God created marriage as the means for those desires to be met.

This is all wonderful news, but it is also difficult news because we live in a world that operates apart from God. This broken world we inhabit has treated this precious gift like nothing but a stupid frat-house joke. It has convinced us that it knows the way to true and lasting sexual pleasure. The blatant hypocrisy of all this is that the world throws us two messages at once: 1) sex is no big deal, and 2) great sex is life's ultimate pleasure, therefore it should be life's highest goal. We have more information about how to make sex better than at any other time in world history, but I have to ask: If the world has discovered the secret to true sexual fulfillment, why do we still get assaulted with all this "new" information? The honest truth is that Satan and the world completely and utterly failed me when it came to sex. When I foolishly decide to listen to what their voices say about sex, they *continue* to fail me. If you keep giving their voices a listening ear, my brothers, they will ultimately fail you too.

An oft-romanticized aspect of masculinity is the notion of a creed, a set of principles that a man will follow to the point of death. Christ-following men are fortunate in this regard. God has our creed laid out for us in his Word. It was written at the dawn of creation before we drew breath. God never promises us a pain-free devotion, but he does tell us that it is a creed we are capable of following. The closer we draw to Christ, the less the command of sexual purity will seem like just another principle to follow. Rather, it becomes a fundamental aspect to our Christian life that we practice to please our Savior, thereby taking a powerful place of honor in our lives.

Yes, it is true that God has high standards. Yes, it is sometimes incredibly difficult to follow those standards. But the rewards that flow from a life in service to those standards renders the world's rewards obsolete. I tried to live without his standards for too many years. Look back at my story. It doesn't work. Look at my story again. Every time I held firm to God's truths about sex was – and continues to be – without a single ounce of regret. When it comes to something as monumental and soul-touching as sex, don't you want to be free of regret and shame? You can be.

Heal us, Father.

Let us see these two gifts through your eyes, and your eyes alone.

Save us from the world.

Save us from ourselves.

OUR WORDS

Life and death are in the power of the tongue . . .
                                                    – Proverbs 18:21

But the things that come out of the mouth come from the heart, and
these make a man 'unclean.'
                                                    – Matthew 15:18

Now that I have talked about achieving purity on the visual side, it's time to discuss the way of purity on the verbal side. I don't have much to say here because the solution is not that difficult or complex. But it still needs to be discussed because we live in an age that is drowning in words. Whether written or spoken, words have more power than we usually choose to acknowledge. When we speak, we rarely think about the ramifications of what comes out of our mouths. When we type cinder-blocks of ranting text message on our phones or online, we rarely pause and consider what the receiver may think or how it may affect them. The Internet, the smartphone revolution and social media have only added to the problem. I am not against these things. They are valuable tools. But, in all honesty, I am still disheartened with what this technology has done to us, not just as a culture, but as human beings living in the same world. It seems that every day I hear about someone using this technology for evil when it is capable of spreading so much good.

When we add feminine beauty into the discussion of words, I have to fight to prevent myself from losing heart. The things that men speak about the beauty of Eve in this day and age are every negative adjective I can think of. The area of sexuality is particularly hideous. The word we use to describe a man who has sex with multiple partners is "normal." The words we use to describe a woman who does the same are "slut," "skank," "hussy" and "whore." No one thinks twice about a man's sexual desires, but a woman who desires sex is called "loose" and "promiscuous." I've heard men claiming to be Christians refer to women who have had premarital sex as "damaged goods." It seems that not a day goes by that I don't see or hear words like this thrown around with reckless abandon by a chuckling chorus.

Men, I have to be blunt here. We have to change the words we use when we talk about and write about female beauty. We have to change the words we use in the presence of women. We have to think twice about the kind of jokes we tell. We *have* to change our words. I'm not just talking about cursing, slurs and slang terms for female anatomy, none of which I need to repeat here. I'm speaking about terms that most people see as socially acceptable, terms like "hottie," "chick," "doll," "bitch." People toss around such terms like candy. I sometimes hear Christ-following men do the tossing (sometimes women are worse than the men). They are tossed around by those who want to show off, gain respect, get a laugh, or embellish an over-the-top ego stroke. Not a single thought is given to the use of these words because their use is so common. But you and I both know that only a mediocre man believes that *common* is the same as *good*. I personally detest such terminology because of how subtly it can cause a man and other men around him to view a woman not as someone, but something. I don't see a single ounce of humanity in them.

Part of the way a man treats a woman with purity, honor and respect is the way he talks around her. If a man truly wants to be a source of life and nobility to women, I don't see why words like the ones I'm talking about have any reason to be a part of his speech, his mind or his heart. A man of nobility knows that a woman is not a smokin' hot chick or a mighty fine piece of fill-in-the-blank. It would not even cross the mind of an honorable man to use foul language around a woman. Some may say, "Just because I use those words about women doesn't mean I *feel* that way." If that's true, then the solution is plain and clear: If you don't feel that way about women, don't use words that suggest you do. Use your words to raise the standard, not bring it lower.

Some may think I'm getting hot under the collar over a minor issue or being too sensitive. That's fine with me. But you and I both live in a sick society that deems many sick things as completely permissible. Our world thinks that all that is gold does in fact glitter. We live in a world that says, "I can say whatever I want!" But we do not belong to the world, men. We belong to God. We were created to protect and honor women with the power of the tongue. Look in God's Word and tell me if you see such words when he talks about his daughters.

Whether it is subtle or overt, the truth remains that women are not being honored and protected by men's words in this world. Men are not using words to build them up. Men are not using words to affirm them. Men are not using words to comfort them, make them feel safe, or simply to compliment them. Instead, I see men using words to manipulate, shame, destroy, intimidate, and violate them. Just spend ten minutes in a comments section on the Internet and you'll see what I mean. It doesn't matter how slightly or humorously the words are used. It all serves the enemy. But in spite of all the collateral damage men cause to women with their words, there is the same reverse side to the darkness.

God designed words to have the power they do because it is with our words that we can pour abundant blessings into the lives of women. I've seen men use their words in beautiful ways when they speak to the women in their lives, beautiful because it is true and from the heart. I've heard husbands say wonderful things about their wives in public settings. One time I overheard my 90-year-old grandpa call my grandma his favorite girl. I can think of times when I wrote one of my lady friends words of encouragement during a difficult time, and how wonderful it felt to imagine their reactions upon receiving them. I can recall times when I've simply said, "I'm here for you." I can think of birthday cards or Mother's Day cards when I had the chance to write how much these specific women matter to me. I can remember times when I prayed over my sisters in Christ. I know other men who do these same things. And I can think of few other things that make me feel more like the man I'm supposed to be. That is the power of words. Let us use them as God intended.

I leave this chapter with some questions:

How do you plan to use your words when you talk or write about women?

Will you choose to use your words as a tool to spread life, joy and peace to God's daughters?

Will you encourage your fellow man to do the same?

Or will you choose to spread death?

What will you choose, my brothers?

A Message To Women

To all my sisters in Christ who have been reading, I want to say thank you. Thank you for reading my story and following me throughout these pages. Thank you for caring about the inner lives of men enough to read a book about what this fight is like from our perspective. I hope it has been illuminating, and above all, healing.

When I started writing this book, it did not initially occur to me to say anything specifically to the ladies. But later on in the process, something from a previous chapter dawned on me: As men and women, we have a responsibility to help one another be the purest we can be *as men* and *as women*. I believe that when it comes to sexual purity, men should be accountable to men only, and women to women only. But as I stated earlier, purity is not all about sex. It is about inspiring one another to honor and respect our genders and not to tear them down with the kind of behavior the world practices. In other words, men can help women be pure and women can help men be pure. What I want to say to you ladies falls in line with this.

Women, as you well know, the world loves to demean, exploit, insult and debase your bodies and your God-designed femininity. Sometimes it's subtle, but mostly, it's flagrant. Whether it's in movies, books, the Internet or TV, men are usually the ones who lead the sinful parade in these areas. Sex trafficking and forced prostitution are the more graphic examples of how some men treat womanhood (I take comfort in the fact that one day, such men will have to stand before the judgment seat of God and give account for these actions). We see this rampant dishonor on a daily basis.

I don't blame women for thinking negatively about men and the current state of masculinity. It is becoming more commonplace to encounter women who are angry at men, have either given up on men, or are just plain indifferent to men. Our society practically shouts to women from the rooftops to feel this way about men. As sad as these realities are, I'm not surprised that they exist. In this dark and cynical age, it is disheartening to see how rare righteous manhood has become. But what is equally disheartening to me is how little most women seem to care.

Something has happened among women in the world today, even women who call themselves Christians, that has contributed mightily to the current state of fallen manhood. Women have contributed one thing above all else: complacency. Rather than viewing men in the light of what they can become through Christ, many women have just come to accept men as they are in their sinful brokenness. But it no longer stops there. These days, such women aren't just accepting the brokenness. They themselves are engaging in it. More and more, I see women bringing themselves to the same base level of the men around them in the name of liberation, self-confidence and individuality. According to the standards of the current androgynous mess that we call gender relations, in order for a woman to be truly free, fully alive and utterly self-confident, she has to be just as vulgar, just as ruthless, just as promiscuous, and just as unfeeling as a man. If a man swears like a sailor around a woman or treats her like an animal, she is not allowed to get offended. If she sleeps with him at night and he leaves her in the morning, she is not supposed to be wounded. If she sees other women being treated this way and eventually acting this way, she is not supposed to call them out on it. Nothing is supposed to bother her. Having a soul is the same as having a weakness. She's not supposed to "judge." She is not supposed to feel. She is not allowed to hurt. She cannot have a heart. In short, she can't be a woman.

Someone needs to explain to me in detail how a woman is better off this way. This does not sound like liberation. It sounds like imprisonment. In the end, that is what it is: imprisonment to a despicably low standard. Why a woman would ever in her right mind want to stoop that low is beyond me. There is no denying that in terms of gender relations, the words *If you can't beat 'em, join 'em* is the rallying cry for many women today. There seems to be this unspoken consensus among women that men will be men and we just have to deal with it, that's just the way it is, it will never change, accept it.

We hear this so much in our culture. But those who walk with God can see right away where that way of thinking comes from. Anything that says nothing in these dark days can ever change for the better is a lie from the mouth of the devil. If God is as big as he says he is, it should not matter to us how much evidence there is to support the enemy's claims. When God said he can make all things new (Revelation 21:5), he meant what he said. That includes the hearts of men and women living in this moment in this culture.

I think many men these days believe that women have no idea what they want in a man. I don't agree. In spite of all the gender confusion flying around, I believe women *do* know what they want men to be. The problem is that American women live in a society that says real men no longer exist, so it's now all up to them. Article after article, book after book, story after story all seem to be saying the same thing: nobility, chivalry, honor and genuine manliness is gone and it isn't coming back. As often as women hear this, I don't think every woman believes it. In spite of the toxicity of our culture, I believe many women still long for the fairytale our world says is dead, for the men of their dreams to be a reality and not a fantasy. I believe women long – even *ache* – for men to be leaders who are pure, sacrificial, tender, caring, loving and noble. I believe you want men to love you first and foremost for *you*.

I write this in the hope that you, my sisters, will believe – will *know* – that such men exist. I tell you the truth when I say that there are men out there who despise the low standard and are fighting to raise it. There are men out there fighting to conquer their fear of what true manhood will bring if they pursue it. There are men out there who long to be noble, who long to win the heart of a woman and make her feel loved, protected, valued, and safe. There are men in the world who want to meet the challenge of loving a woman's heart more than her body. There are men out there who want to be married, who want to be good husbands and want to be good fathers. I'm not describing men who only exist in the ancient pages of mythology. I'm describing real men.

On behalf of all the righteous men in the world today, I make this request to you women: Don't give up on us. Please. Don't listen to the voice of the world that constantly tells you that men will never be anything other than idiots and eternal adolescents that you can never love, rely on, or trust. It is a lie. There are men out there who want to be – and *can* be – what God has called them to be.

You can help us, ladies.

We need you to tell us that we matter to you.

We need you to tell us from your hearts that you believe we can become the men God calls us to be.

We need your help.

We need your love.

We need your grace.

We need you.

I want to close with one more thing. I admit it's probably not necessary at this point, but, in all honesty, I care too much to *not* say it. I wish I could tell this to every woman out there in person, but I think this will do.

When God made you a woman, he knew exactly what he was doing. He did not make a mistake. He was – and is – in awe of you. He wants you to wake up every day, look in the mirror, and say, "I'm so happy to be your daughter." When you think to yourself, "I am a woman," your Father doesn't want you to cringe. He wants you to smile. God does not want you to try to be a man. You aren't. You can't. You never will be. You are a woman. That is not something to apologize for. It is not something to hate about yourself for the rest of your life. It is a sacred honor. Your feminine heart and all that comes with it is not something to bury, kill or wish away. It is what makes you who you are, and it is something that is more precious to God than you will ever know. The longings you carry in your soul matter, my sisters. *They matter.* You are not weak if you long for a good man to pursue you and love you all the days of your life. You are not less of a woman for wanting marital love and motherhood instead of a career. You are not less of a woman for wanting to serve God wholeheartedly by remaining single.

The world is wrong. The world has no idea what a true woman really is. But God does.

He values you.

He loves you.

And he wants your heart.

Parting Thoughts

For a while now, I've wanted to have the chance to visit a group of women who I encountered during a certain time in my life. These are women who I still remember quite clearly. But when I saw them during this particular time, I was only looking with my physical eyes for reasons too unpleasant for me to want to remember. These women are part of a group that never should have existed in the first place. They are all the women I have ever lusted after. These women were forsaken, dishonored, taken for granted, and viewed as nothing more than products by me, a man who knew full well that what he was doing was devastating to the heart of his Father. Many men indulge in lust without believing their actions are wrong. Not me. I *knew* it was sin. I *knew* it devastated my Savior and wounded his heart. I did it anyway. If I had that chance, that chance to visit each member of this group in person, I would take that opportunity to say one thing: "I am so sorry."

There is another group of women as well, another group I have wanted to visit. I saw these women at a time in my life I will never forget. It was during a time in which I stood on the heights of unprecedented joy, thanksgiving, and freedom. This group of women acted as a powerful guide into this ongoing season of my life. They are all the women who used their beauty to draw me back to God. These women posed for paintings hundreds of years ago. They posed for artistic photographs. They allowed their bodies to be immortalized in sculpture. In allowing themselves to become art, this special group of women spoke (and still speak) this to my heart: "We bear the image of the one who gave us this captivating beauty. We were knit together in the secret place. Our beauty is sacred. It was set apart for a holy purpose. We were not made to fulfill you.

We are shadows. We are dim reflections. Our beauty is a message from the Source of all beauty. Do not go to us. Go to him, for he is inviting you to life. This is who we are. We are women. Honor us." If I had that chance, that chance to visit each individual woman in this group, I would take that opportunity to say one thing: "Thank you."

Writing this book was not so much a decision as it was a need. I *needed* to tell you about my journey, my war, my redemption, and all that God taught me for two reasons: to let you know that enduring freedom from lust is truly possible, and to call you to arms as courageous men of Christ to declare war on this sin that has held too many men captive for far too long. For it is a war we are fighting, men. And we are not meant to fight this war alone. I don't want to believe Satan's lie that I am the only one seeking to destroy lust before it claims one more life. I don't want to believe I am alone. I believed I was alone for too many years. I listened to too many wrong voices. I bought too many lies. I dishonored too many women. No more. I am tolling the bell. It's time for war. And I need you.

There's a scene from one of my all-time favorite stories that speaks to the soul of all I've been talking about. Our hero was born into a wealthy kingdom, only to have his father, the king of the land, killed by a jealous rival. He is exiled and forbidden to return. He meets a couple aimless individuals that show him a lifestyle without sorrow and pain. But something that starts out as healing and helpful turns into something disastrous: he grows to adulthood in a life of comfort and ease. Pleasure is the greatest goal in this life, a life that asks and requires nothing of him. He is taught that responsibility and true life are not things to be sought after. Why bring all that pain and worry into your life? He spends years living this way until finally, one starry night, when he sees what his life has become, the spirit of his dead father comes to him.

– Simba. You have forgotten me.
– No! How could I?
– You have forgotten who you are, and so have forgotten me. Look inside yourself, Simba. You are more than what you have become. You must take your place in the circle of life.

– How can I go back? I'm not who I used to be!
– Remember who you are. You are my son, and the one true king.
Remember who you are.

This moment in *The Lion King* is powerful for many reasons, but I think the main reason it is so profound – and also why the story resonates so deeply with men in particular – is that it reveals what many of us don't want to admit. This moment speaks to the current state of manhood in our world today: boys without fathers who spend their days existing instead of living, seeking their own pleasure while forsaking a world that desperately needs them. It is downright tragic. And we know it. We know something has gone terribly wrong in the lives of men. In some way, every man on Earth is like Simba: born into a kingdom where the king promises great reward, only to have it taken from us by the evil one. We shape our lives so that we don't have to fight for anyone's hearts or worry about the trials of authentic, God-defined masculinity. God comes into our lives by any means necessary and tells us the same things Mufasa does: *This is not you. You are made for so much more. You are my son. You are a king.* What does Simba do? He sees the truth, and the truth sets him free. He returns, fights, and reclaims all that was lost. This same glory can happen for us . . . if we would only act.

Some of you may be saying, "But you don't know what I've done." You're right. I don't know. But God does. And he is still after you. He looks at you and does not define you by the crumbling ruins of your life. No. He sees the noble son beneath the mire. He sees your true worth and your true value. He sent his one and only son to die in your place to show you just how much your worth means to him. Hold to that truth, my brothers. Hold it like a lifeline. Do not spend another moment of your life believing you are beyond redemption. God has mastered the art of second chances. It doesn't matter how far you've fallen. Deuteronomy 31:6 says that God will never leave us or forsake us. In other words, he is not giving up on you. No matter how difficult, you can take back what was stolen. When you do, you will see that there is no other life worth pursuing than a life heart-to-heart, step-by-step, and side-to-side with Jesus. All we have to do is choose.

What I failed to understand for so long was this astonishingly basic truth of choice. As a man, I make the choice to follow Christ and let him be the guide of my life. As his follower, it is up to me. Others can serve as mentors, but I am the one who must choose a holy life. Am I going to succeed in being sin-free for the rest of my life? No. At this point you expect me to say, "But of course. I'm only human." But I won't say that. I will not encourage *you* to say that, either. That is the voice of mediocrity. It is the indignant utterance of mediocre men all around the world, men who have accepted their brokenness and decided to live with it. Yes, we cannot fully escape the curse of the Fall. Yes, we are born into the world as sinners. But we were not created to *be* sinners. We were not created to live by the ways of a fallen world. Brothers, you and I are more than that. We are followers of Christ, and he calls to us with the voice of authenticity. The voice of authenticity tells us that we cannot use our broken humanity as an excuse to remain imprisoned by the sinful nature. It is not an excuse to ignore change. Christ tells us throughout the gospel time and again, "Yes, you are broken. But you do not have to stay that way."

We simply cannot allow ourselves to forget that every time we sin, whether we are aware of it or not, we do it because we choose to do so. We cannot blame our fallen humanity. We cannot blame our culture. We cannot blame others. The mediocre man makes excuses to justify his sinful choices. The son of God knows he has no one to blame but himself. As it is our choice to be slaves, it is also our choice to be free. Choosing freedom is not always easy. But it is that much more difficult when you are not united with Christ in an intimate, ever-growing bond of lifelong relationship. When I am close to him, I *want* to please him by not giving in to temptation. As his beloved son, it is the desire of my heart to bless him with my choices. Forsaking lust for freedom is the choice we have always had before us.

This freedom has always existed.

It is time to choose it.
It is time to be free.

> It is for freedom that Christ has set us free. Stand firm, then, and do not let yourselves be burdened again by a yoke of slavery (Galatians 5:1).

I know you are out there, men. I want you standing with me as we make a stand and fight to reclaim and protect the naked soul of feminine beauty, a beauty that is closer to God's heart than we can ever imagine. What I am asking you to do is dangerous. As I write these words, I face the enemy's assaults almost daily. So do you. The voice of the world is a powerful voice, and most of the time it seems more truthful than the voice of our King. We know people who serve the world. We know what it's like to serve the world. If you choose to fight this war, opposition from the world will come. Temptation will come. You will be opposed for the rest of your lives because Satan hates you. He fears you. And he will do whatever it takes to keep you imprisoned. He will tell you that your pleasure and your comfort matters above all else. He will tell you that you are all alone. He will tell you that making the changes needed to become a man is too hard. He is the accuser. He is the father of lies. He never sleeps. He never waits. He will never stop speaking to you. He will never stop hunting you. It will be this way until you die. The rewards gleaned from a life of purity are too great for this to be an easy road.

Together, I want us as men to rise to the holy standards that God has placed before us and make those standards unshakable truths of our lives until the day God takes us home.

I want to see your hearts and your lives set free from lust.

I am for you, men. I am your ally.

You are not alone in this fight.

We can do this together.

We can unite as brothers under a banner of righteousness.

We can be heroes.

We can be men.

We can walk this earth and live this life with "not even a hint of sexual immorality."

We can do this because God says we can do it.

We can work to create a world where men will never say, "I wonder what she looks like naked," but will say instead, "How can I see her and love her like Christ does?"

We can work to create a world where a woman can see a man looking at her and she can smile, because she will know that it is God he is truly seeing.

There's some good in this world, men. And it's worth fighting for.

Will you stand with me?

> Not that I have already obtained all this, or have already arrived at my goal, but I press on to take hold of that for which Christ Jesus took hold of me. Brothers and sisters, I do not consider myself yet to have taken hold of it. But one thing I do: Forgetting what is behind and straining toward what is ahead, I press on toward the goal to win the prize for which God has called me heavenward in Christ Jesus.
> – Philippians 3:12-14

> I run in the path of your commands, for you have set my heart free.
> – Psalm 119:32

EPILOGUES

Prayers

In the morning, LORD, you hear my voice;
in the morning I lay my requests before you
and wait in expectation.

– Psalm 5:3

The prayer of a righteous man is powerful and effective.

– James 5:16

I have listed here a series of prayers that I have used in various situations. These prayers have had a tremendous benefit in reminding me of who I am as a son of God, where the real battle lies, and assuring me that I must not let my freedom give way to slavery. None of these prayers are set in stone. Each one has variations and alternations. If you have your own prayers for such times, that is wonderful. I want you to pray as you feel led. All I want to do here is offer what I use in my own life.

Though we all differ in how we pray, we can all certainly agree on one thing: We must never forget what is available to us through honest and heartfelt prayer. God has given us great authority and power over lust through this mighty gift. As free men, we must use it for our behalf and the behalf of others. My hope is that the prayers I offer here will bless your lives in the way they have blessed mine.

The prayer below is one that I find myself being led to pray more and more. I have used it whenever I encounter a woman in life or in an image whose beauty moves me. She might be a celebrity. It could be a woman on a magazine cover, a woman posing for art, a woman I see in passing, a co-worker or a friend. Ninety-nine percent of this prayer is pure Scripture. Praying Scripture is truly powerful. Nothing compares to speaking the very Word of God over a woman you see.

This prayer accomplishes these things for me: 1) It reminds me not to ignore, disregard, or dismiss her beauty: 2) It helps me admire her beauty as a gift from God instead of lusting after it to satisfy my own sinful desires: 3) It reminds me that she needs God more than anything else on Earth. The passages of Scripture that make up the majority of this prayer have been huge in helping me grow in honor and appreciation of feminine beauty. I hope it will do the same for you.

O Lord, my Lord,
Let me hear her voice;
let me see her face,
for her voice is sweet
and her face is lovely.
She has stolen my heart, Lord Jesus;
she has stolen my heart
with one glance of her eyes.
Like a lily among thorns
is this maiden before me.
I praise you, O Lord.
I praise you because she is
fearfully and wonderfully made;
more precious than rubies is she.
Quiet her with love;
rejoice over her with singing.
Allure her, O Lord, allure her.
Lead her into the desert
and speak tenderly to her.
Make her lie down in green pastures;
lead her beside quiet waters.
Set her feet in a spacious place.

O Lord, my Lord,
Create in her a pure heart;
create in her the unfading beauty
of a gentle and quiet spirit.
May her soul find rest in you alone,
for your yoke is easy
and your burden is light.
O Lord, my Lord,
How majestic is your name in all the earth!
I praise you because she is
fearfully and wonderfully made.

God, thank you so much.
Thank you, God, that she is a human being who bears your holy image.
Thank you for creating her to be so beautiful.
Thank you for her female body, her beauty,
her grace and her sensuality.
You created her to be this beautiful. Her beauty was your idea.
This is true of her because it is true of you.
Help me to see this woman with your eyes,
to see what you see, Jesus.
Please protect me from worshiping her instead of you.
I don't long for her beauty. I long for your beauty.
You are so beautiful.
You are so artistic.
You are so sensual.
You are so captivating.
You are so precious.
Please reveal what you are trying to tell me through her beauty.
Thank you for using this woman's beauty to draw me to you.
I worship your holy name.
I give you all honor, glory and praise.

This next prayer is more in the vein of healing and spiritual warfare. As I have mentioned, we as men need to be reminded continuously of the fact that every woman we see is a human being. She is a real person. She has a story. She has hurts. She has feelings. She is hated by the enemy. And she is loved by God. When men come to God in prayer on behalf of a woman – even if we don't know her – we are living out an amazing part of what God created men to do. Most women long to be honored, protected and fought for by men. Going to war on her behalf through the power of prayer is a way to assure that those things happen. What an awesome privilege.

I bring this woman before you, Jesus.
I recognize that she is a human being.
You love her more than I will ever know.
Jesus, I don't know her. I don't know her story. I don't know her life.
But you do, Lord. You know everything about her.
I pray for her protection, Jesus.
Protect her from the ways of the enemy.
I pray that she will come to know you as I know you.
Bring people into her life to help her see you for who you truly are, Lord Jesus.
May she realize the power of her feminine beauty.
May she use her body as an instrument of purity and righteousness.
Heal her wounds. Heal her brokenness. Heal her damaged heart.
In the name of Jesus Christ, I renounce Satan's claim over her.
Satan, in the name of Jesus Christ, I command you to flee from her.
I place her under the rule, the protection and authority of Jesus Christ.
She is not yours, Satan. I renounce any claims you have over her life in the name of Jesus.
I cast you back into the pit of hell in the name of Jesus Christ.
May no weapon formed against her succeed.
May she never use her beauty for your evil deeds ever again.
Jesus, bring her your peace that passes beyond all understanding.
Guide her back to the ways of her heart, Lord God.

Move her in profound ways that touch her soul.
Romance her, Lord God.
I thank you for giving me this chance to be a man of honor.
I worship you and honor your holy name.

   This is something I've had to pray when the enemy tries to lie
to me and tempt me with lust. The previous prayers do collateral
damage to Satan's tactics, but sometimes you have to fight harder.
You will have to be relentless when you pray this prayer. You will
have to be relentless because Satan is relentless. You may have to
do this multiple times a day. But the more times you pray this, the
faster Satan and lust will flee from you.

I renounce you, Satan.
I renounce you, Lust.
I renounce and I break the claims you have on my life.
Satan, your power over me is broken.
I place the saving power of Jesus Christ between you and me.
He died for my sins on the cross.
He was raised from the dead.
He has conquered sin and death.
He has conquered you, Satan. And I will conquer you.
For I am his son.
You will not defile this temple any longer.
I will not believe your lies any longer.
I am not a prisoner. I am not a slave. I am free.
I am free because Christ set me free.
I am a temple of the living God.
I am not my own. I belong to Jesus.
My body is an instrument of purity and righteousness.
I cast you back into the pit of hell in the name of Jesus Christ.
Get out.

This is something to pray whenever memories of lustful escapades come to the surface. This is something that must be prayed as often and relentless as necessary. Memories are powerful. In the case of lust, those memories may never leave. It has been my primary battleground ever since I was set free. I can still recall lustful images and videos with perfect clarity. How I wish this was not so. Nighttime is a particularly vulnerable time for my thought life. It is all too easy to let your guard down when all you care about is sleep. Before I go to bed I have needed to cover my time of sleep and even my dreams in prayer. It has been enormously helpful. The prayer below has continued to help me overcome whatever sinful residue is trapped in my mind whenever it rears its ugly head. May it be the same for you.

Lord Jesus, I do not want these memories anymore.
These memories are such an evil distraction from the truth.
These memories tell me I am not free. This is a lie. I am free forever.
The life I desire will not be found in these memories.
It is found in you.
And so right now, right here, I release to you every woman I have ever lusted after.
I place each of those women into your hands.
I release to you whatever memories I am deliberately holding onto.
I acknowledge the beauty of these women, Lord.
Their beauty is your beauty.
You love those women with all your heart, Lord Jesus.
I pray that all the women I ever lusted after will come to know you as I do.
Save them as you have saved me.
I consecrate my mind to you, Lord Jesus.
By the power of your Holy Spirit, transform and renew my mind.
I consecrate my thought life and my imagination to your holy name.
I reject these memories in favor of the truth of your Word.

Thank you, Jesus, for all that you accomplished on the cross.
Thank you, Jesus, that I am no longer burdened by a yoke of slavery.
I am free. I belong to you. I am your son. You are my father.
I worship your holy name.

Prayer is an incredibly powerful weapon, men. It is essential to the Christian life like water and air is to the body. It is – and always has been – one of the most formidable tools in our arsenal against the forces of darkness. Just remember: pray *with* your heart and *from* your heart. When you and I pray, we have to pray with everything: body, mind, soul, spirit, heart, speech. Don't just talk to the air or mull it over in your mind. Half-hearted prayer leads to half-hearted results. Don't make mediocrity the standard of your prayer life. Find a place with no distractions whatsoever and engage. *Engage* with God. *Engage* in warfare. Get other brothers in the faith to engage with you. The Lord hears your prayers, men. He knows your hearts. God will fully honor your desire to honor, protect and fight for women, all of whom he holds close to his heart like a satchel of jewels. Make prayer your lifestyle. Make warfare a priority. You will receive rewards too abundant to count.

Prayer request

Since we are talking about prayer, I have one further prayer challenge for us as men: Pray for women who struggle with pornography addiction.

This is a book about men's struggles with lust, and I've spoken at length about porn in these pages. But the oft-neglected truth is that porn is not just a man's problem. It is a *human* problem. It is not a new struggle for women, either. It has been going on for longer than most of us know. These struggling women are far more common than we realize. Many of them sit in church with us. Some of us are married to them. A lot of them are coworkers. We may even know them personally. And they are not receiving all the help they need to be free. The church has been silent for too long, and many women feel they have to fight this battle alone. God's daughters who struggle with pornography addiction don't need pity. They don't need scorn. They don't need confusion. They need compassion. They need grace. They need to know that they are not alone. They need other women to fight *for* them and *with* them.

Thankfully, the conversation is starting and resources are slowly beginning to appear. But it needs to happen faster. Brothers, we know that being addicted to pornography is no lightweight matter. Many of us know what this addiction is capable of. We know full well what it can do to ruin us on the outside and the inside. It does the exact same thing to women. It is just as dangerous, just as mind-altering, and just as life-destroying.

I don't want our sisters in Christ to be in bondage for one more day to pornography addiction. And so we need to pray. Pray that they receive accountability from women close to them or struggling with them. Pray that they will not suffer silently but have the courage to confess their struggle to a woman whom they can trust. Pray that a resource will appear that they have access to for healing. Pray that their identities will not be defined by this struggle, but by the words of their Father. Pray that they find fulfillment and rescue in their Father alone.

For those women reading this, I wish to say one thing to you: The same freedom I've spoken about in this book to my brothers is there for you, too. Don't believe Satan's lie that you're too dirty or unclean to seek the help you need. You can be healed. Your lives and your minds can be restored by your Father in heaven. Don't give up. You can be free.

There is always hope.

To singles

I'm not writing this little letter here to those who have willingly chosen to remain single for various reasons. I am writing this to those like me: single, and longing for marriage.

When I began this book, I was close to turning 26. As of this writing, I'm close to turning 29. One thing remains: I'm still single. The way I feel about it also remains. Yes, some days I am completely happy and wholly content in my singleness. Yes, there are times when I am able to fully trust God and rest in the assurance of his promises. Yes, there are days when being single is so amazing that I could see myself being a confirmed bachelor for life.

But mostly, I don't like it. Sometimes, I even hate it. I know I'm not alone in this.

Brothers and sisters, there is simply no getting around it. Waiting for a mate is hard. *It's hard.* It isn't just hard, either. It's painful.

For most of my life I have loved going to weddings. I loved sharing in the joy of the newlyweds even if I didn't know them very well. I used to look forward to them as the date drew near. Nowadays, it's a different story. Nowadays, I have to try to be enthusiastic about a wedding. The hopeful romantic you read about in the previous chapters no longer looks forward to weddings. Mostly, I have little to no desire to go when I'm invited. Why the change in outlook? Because it hurts. It hurts to repeatedly see others experiencing this gift of marriage that I have ached for almost all my life – and still don't have.

I've heard people – well-meaning people, mind you – use many of the same standard lines to help ease the pain and hardship of waiting throughout my life. They may sound familiar to you (I particularly hate the last one): *Singleness is a gift. Learn how to be content. Your single years are valuable. Be happy for those that are married even though you aren't. You're still young. It's not too late. Don't worry, it'll happen when it happens.* When people tell me these things, they aren't wrong. I know these things to be true. I also know that when my heart is in a state of longing, these truths couldn't be more meaningless. But aside from the hardship of waiting, my singleness has taught me something else: if there is one thing that is even harder and more painful to do that wait, it's to hope.

We live in an increasingly hopeless society. Hopelessness is especially prevalent in regards to the state of relationships and marriage. Many believe that American society is post-marriage, that marriage in America is basically irrelevant. Given the divorce rate, and the fact that men and women seem to be growing more suspicious of and cynical towards one another every passing day, I don't blame people for losing heart. I myself go through occasional bouts of hopelessness that feel inescapable. I look at my life and I see no chance of finding a wife. The enemy, of course, leaps on this like a pack of wolves. *You've been singe your whole life, so what makes you think the rest of it is going to be any different? No woman is ever going to reciprocate your affections. No woman is going to love you back. No woman cares about wanting to love a man well. They only care about what you can give them, and you can't give them much. Don't you get it? Women don't give a damn about men anymore! Nothing's going to change, Scott. Give up and stop torturing yourself.*

These episodes used to be commonplace. But I don't have these bouts of hopelessness that often anymore. They have mostly vanished. You see, the Lord taught me something a few months ago that has consistently saved me from despair, and still does to this day: to give up hope for her is to give up faith in God.

One thing I have tried to do at various times in my life is to stop hoping for a mate. I've tried to tell myself something like this: "It's not going to happen anytime soon, maybe never, so just move on with your life." I tried to make an agreement with this statement because it felt realistic and logical. It put me in control of the situation. My

Scott J. Einig

acceptance of the fact that marriage was not going to happen was a way of dulling the pain of longing. I don't do this anymore. I didn't see how foolish it was back then as I do now. You see, nothing I did made that longing go away. Nothing. Work, busyness, vacation, social time with friends and family, self-imposed distractions . . . none of it took the desire away. Not even prayer took it away. Even when I asked God to remove the longing for a wife, it was still there the next day. What does all this mean? It means that this desire that God put in my heart is there for a reason. I've come to believe that the primary reason is to teach me how to hope.

The word defines faith as "being sure of what we hope for and certain of what we do not see" (Hebrews 11:1). We tend to interpret this verse in light of Christianity as a whole. We can't see God, but we have faith in him. I think this passage also applies to the desires of our hearts. I sometimes think about my own desires, and some of them seem far-fetched and outright impossible. And then God reminds me: "I'm bigger than your desires." I look at my longing for a mate, and I have to constantly remind myself that it is not my job to ask, "How is this possibly going to happen?" My job is to trust that this is a good desire. My job is to trust that my Father does in fact care about it. My job is to trust that he will provide. My job is to seek God first in all things. My job is to become a man. My job is to hope.

I write this to you, my fellow singles, to encourage you when you feel that same hopelessness rising in your hearts. Not a week goes by where I don't think about and pray for you in your longings for a mate. Remember: following the Gospel of Cynicism is easy. Making agreements with the enemy is easy. But to have the faith to hope when there is no reason for that hope? That's hard. And that's the place where God works the mightiest. It's in that place of internal suffering where we develop "perseverance; perseverance, character; and character, hope" (Romans 5:3-4). When we have this kind of faith – when we trust God like this with longings this deep – we are free to be forged into the people we need to be. We need to be people who need him more than anything else. That's the kind of woman I want to spend the rest of my life with.

Let us seek our Father with all our hearts.
Let us become who we need to be.
Let us become who God created us to be.
Let us do this before we get married.

> But the eyes of the Lord are on those who fear him, on those whose hope is in his unfailing love,
> to deliver them from death and keep them alive in famine.
> We wait in hope for the Lord; he is our help and our shield.
> In him our hearts rejoice, for we trust in his holy name.
> May your unfailing love rest upon us, O Lord, even as we put our hope in you.
>
> - Psalm 33:18-22

> There is surely a hope for you, and your hope will not be cut off.
>
> - Proverbs 23:18

> For everything that was written in the past was written to teach us, so that through endurance and the encouragement of the Scriptures we might have hope.
>
> - Romans 15:4

- April 2018

To my brothers and sisters. . .

If there is one thing my war taught me, it is how much I need others to have victory over the enemy. I've seen the power of God work mightily in his people when they refuse to fight their battles alone. So in the interest of remaining united, I invite you to keep the conversation going with me. I want to hear from you. I want to hear your stories, your testimonies, your trials, your tribulations and your victories. I want to be built up by your faith. Whether you are 12 or 90, single or married, American or Chinese, I want to be taught by you and learn from what God has done and is doing for you.

Write to me at throughtheartistseyes@hotmail.com so that we may keep the talk, the action, the prayers, and the healing alive and well. I may not be able to reply to every email, but know that your words won't go unread. Remember, brothers and sisters: We aren't meant to walk the journey of the Christian life alone. We are all in this together.

> As iron sharpens iron, so one person sharpens another
> – Proverbs 27:17

> And above all these virtues put on love, which binds them all together in perfect unity.
> – Colossians 3:14

About the Author

Scott J. Einig is a non-professional yet highly passionate author, artist, poet, and devoted lover of Jesus Christ. He is currently based near Seattle, Washington. This is his first book.